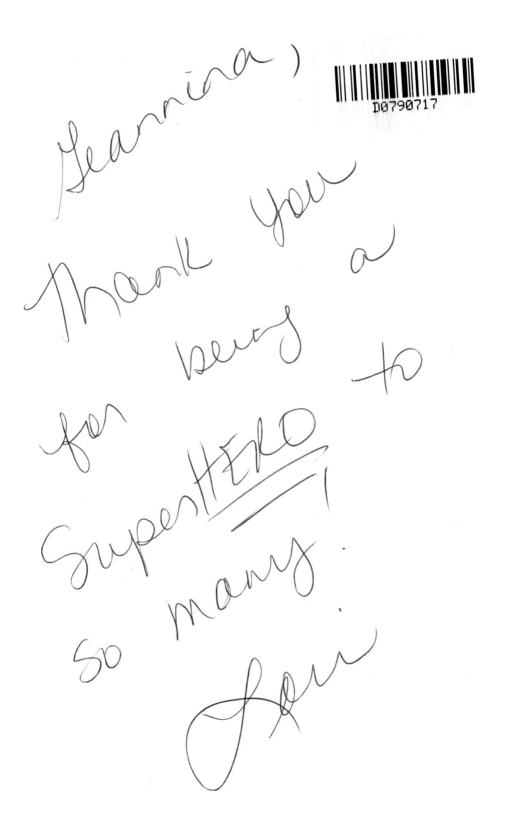

Jeannina,

Thank you
for being a
Superhero to
so many.

Lori

SOS!

Save Our Students

Solutions for Schools, Staff, Students,
Stakeholders, & Society

LORI BITAR

Education Expert and Super-HERO

ISBN: 978-1-4834-5709-3 (sc)
ISBN: 978-1-4834-5707-9 (e)

Library of Congress Control Number: 2013923497

Because of the dynamic nature of the Internet, any web addresses or links contained in this book may have changed since publication and may no longer be valid. The views expressed in this work are solely those of the author and do not necessarily reflect the views of the publisher, and the publisher hereby disclaims any responsibility for them.

Any people depicted in stock imagery provided by Thinkstock are models, and such images are being used for illustrative purposes only.
Certain stock imagery © Thinkstock.

Lulu Publishing Services rev. date: 7/27/2016

To all of the true superheroes—my students!
I can't express in words how all of you made
me feel along the way. Thank you!

Thank you for choosing to join me on this journey by reading my book. I never planned on writing it, but so many teachers and adults I encountered in my work were inspired and motivated by my stories about my students that they continued to tell me that I should write a book. So, here it is. I truly wanted to convey the gravity of the current state of education and empower adults with the knowledge that every interaction they have with a child has the power to change the entire trajectory of the youth's life. If I wrote a book, I wanted to find a way to help anyone working with kids discover ways to own their own behavior and change it if needed. I also wanted to provide resources that were not readily available in a format that was easy to use and enjoyable to read. After many readings and much feedback from a variety of audiences, I hope that this final product accomplishes what I set out to do. It turns out that most people who read the book tell me that, "EVERYBODY SHOULD READ THIS BOOK". I think so too and hope that you will spread the word and join my growing Super-HERO team.

Each chapter tells the story of one of my student sidekicks and provides lessons learned along the way. The individual chapters identify archenemies commonly faced in education and other non-profit sectors, provide useful resources, and guide readers to examine their own behaviors to determine how they impact a student's learning and overall well-being:

- **H:** Do your actions/behaviors *help*, not *hinder*?
- **E:** Do your actions/behaviors *engage*, not *exclude*?
- **R:** Do your actions/behaviors *resuscitate*, not *ruin*?
- **O:** Do your actions/behaviors *overjoy*, not *obliterate*?

Due to recent adoption of the new Every Student Succeeds Act, teachers are tasked with teaching social-emotional skills to students without having had the training and opportunity to develop their own social-emotional skills in the workplace. As you are tasked to give away something you might not yet have, I have aligned and delineated how CASEL'S five competencies are woven throughout the book. The new law asks for these skills to be included in accountability measures and school grades so it is more important than ever to start a conversation and provide training and support on this issue. I am in the process of developing and designing classroom kits, professional development, and additional adult and children's books on this topic and hope you will consider these to include in your toolkit. Here are CASEL'S five competencies in Social Emotional Learning:

- **Self-awareness:** The ability to accurately recognize one's emotions and thoughts and their influence on behavior. This includes accurately assessing one's strengths and limitations and possessing a well-grounded sense of confidence and optimism.
- **Self-management:** The ability to regulate one's emotions, thoughts, and behaviors effectively in different situations. This includes managing stress, controlling impulses, motivating oneself, and setting and working toward achieving personal and academic goals.
- **Social awareness:** The ability to take the perspective of and empathize with others from diverse backgrounds and cultures, to understand social and ethical norms for behavior, and to recognize family, school, and community resources and supports.
- **Relationship skills:** The ability to establish and maintain healthy and rewarding relationships with diverse individuals and groups. This includes communicating clearly, listening actively, cooperating, resisting inappropriate social pressure, negotiating conflict constructively, and seeking and offering help when needed.
- **Responsible decision making:** The ability to make constructive and respectful choices about personal behavior and social interactions based on consideration of ethical standards, safety concerns, social norms, the realistic evaluation of consequences of various actions, and the well-being of self and others.

In the chapters that follow, as you review a student-sidekick story, use the guide at the end of each section to reframe, shape, and unleash specific and intentional behaviors and social emotional competencies to meet the needs of youth who need your help.

CONTENTS

DEFINITION OF A SUPERHERO

Merriam-Webster.com defines *superhero* as "a fictional hero having extraordinary or superhuman powers; *also*: an exceptionally skillful or successful person." Traditional superheroes have a few similar characteristics, many of which are applicable to all those who support struggling youth.

- **Strong and Brave:** Big superheroes seem to be overwhelmingly male, but when big muscles or a soldier's training aren't required, women are slightly more likely than men to take death-defying risks to help others. Feminine heroics are private, fueled by empathy rather than displays of prowess—think Harriet Tubman or Mother Teresa. Many of the teachers and adults who work with youth I know have strength and bravery beyond compare.
- **Intelligent:** Teachers make an average of five hundred decisions per day. They are also required to hold multiple degrees and attend ongoing learning opportunities every year for the newest initiatives.
- **Respected Role Model:** In a contest, people were invited to create six-word essays about educators and mentors who were meaningful to them. Answers like "I remember her fifty years later," "Selflessly dedicated to someone else's success," and "They doubted, you believed, I succeeded", illustrate the special powers that youth workers often exhibit.
- **Wears a Costume:** Anyone who has worked in a classroom setting knows that the following items are costume essentials: flat shoes for running around all day, comfortable pants for sitting on the floor and playing kickball at recess, modest shirt, and special super-HERO glasses that see the good in every student encountered.
- **Has a Sidekick:** My student sidekicks over the years have taught me more than I could have ever imagined about being a true super-HERO.

- **Has a Weakness (Kryptonite):** Youth workers can have many, but our biggest is probably caring too much. We have much to learn and experience a tremendous amount of stress daily that would have to rank off the charts on the scale of stress and burnout. It is our most difficult challenge to manage and navigate the interactions and instructional delivery in the tyranny of the moment each day in the classroom without "losing it".

- **Uses Gadgets:** As we train students for jobs and careers that haven't even been invented, we use iPads, laptops, tablets, gizmos, whiteboards, LCD projectors, center-based games and activities, books, games, and treasure chests, and the ultimate equalizer-the hug.

- **Has an Archenemy:** Education and social service agencies have many archenemies to battle: federal rules, state rules, district rules, the building principal's rules, demanding parents, and societal conditions like poverty, abuse, neglect, gangs, and media influences. The tyranny of the moment is always present and the conflicting mandates and initiatives passed by leaders who have lost touch with the classroom environment have overburdened many to the point of fight or flight.

- **Has a Lair or Hideout:** The true "bat cave" of a teacher is the classroom.

- **Secret Identity (Alter Ego):** Although many believe it to be true, we don't have a bed hiding in the classroom. We have a real life outside the classroom too!

- **Has a Goal and Is Determined:** There is probably no one on the planet who can understand, write, and measure goals better than a youth workers. Teachers write lesson plans and unit plans that start with "The student will be able to" and continue on with measureable learning goals, behavior goals, individual goals, and class goals. Even their own professional goals are part of their development plan. Youth workers keep track of data, goals, targets, and progress towards grant and program outcomes on a daily basis. As for determination, the character of many youth workers is unwavering and tenacious as they work to fight for kids everywhere.

The book and documentary, _Waiting for "Superman"_, enlightened many to the state of education today. As the book's back cover proclaims, "The American public school system is in crisis, failing millions of students, producing almost as many dropouts as graduates, and threatening our economic future. By 2020, the United States will have 123 million high-skill jobs to fill—and fewer than 50 million Americans qualified to fill them." My hope is that this book will advance and awaken that knowledge in stakeholders and supporters across all sectors of society so that we can activate and coordinate our talents to acknowledge the strength, wisdom, and power *we already have* to make a difference every day. There is no need to wait for anybody, anywhere.

You are already a super-HERO. It's time to unleash your superpowers.

Education is the most powerful weapon
which you can use to change the world.
—Nelson Mandela

How It All Began

Me, Fighting for My Life

- **The Motto:** The lyrics from Kirk Franklin's "Looking for you" describe how he had been down so long that he never thought he would see the light of day. My childhood and life challenges along the way were filled with darkness and despair and I felt many times that I wouldn't see the light of day as I struggled through my fear and hurt. I was always looking for a HERO or a sidekick to be there for me to find a way out.
- **The Sidekick:** None available
- **The Archenemies:** Alcoholism and Violence
- **The Kryptonite:** Youth, isolation, fear, poverty, loneliness, abuse, my family history
- **The Super-HERO Lesson:** It only takes a minute to intervene and make an impact!
- **Social Emotional Learning Competency: Relationship skills**

My mother's family settled on a farm in Big Neck, Illinois. It was a rural community straight out of the old-time show *Hee Haw*. There were nine children in the family who needed schooling during the winter months when farming was limited. Violence erupted often, and the words they used toward each other were demeaning, demoralizing, and destructive. Although the life they lived was full of strife and grit, my Grandmother worked as the teacher in the one room schoolhouse to try to ensure her kids could find a better way of life. Education was always important to her—maybe she felt like it was the only way out of difficult circumstances. She was a resilient woman, demanding and purposeful when she believed that a child needed help.

My Grandfather would often use violence and verbal abuse as tools to keep Grandma from moving forward in her personal mission, but she was a super-HERO in her own right and would use her grit to get up and fight to go another day for the kids. She drove the bus for the special-education students for a while and served as a district PTA supervisor for many years after teaching in the one room schoolhouse. She continued her push for education with me over the years and told me repeatedly, "get your education, get your education." Of course, that drove me nuts most of the time and I dismissed what she had to say until I got much older.

My mother kicked, screamed, and fought her way out of my Grandparents' house as quickly as she possibly could. She had incredible talents and gifts for science, athletics, and teaching. Her scholarship to college and her dream of becoming a scientist quickly evaporated as she made a series of bad decisions that impacted us all. The violent husbands, alcoholism, and factory work that scarred and burned her hands sent her life on a rapidly deteriorating cycle. After a concussion and a six-week coma, numerous holiday beatings, and police visits for domestic violence, she found a way to finish her college degree and major in, of all things, education! Maybe she felt like it was the only way out of difficult circumstances and her way to continue her mother's education super-HERO legacy.

As I was growing up, our family life was full of violence and strife. By the time I was four years old, I had seen numerous violent altercations, had been served alcohol often, and had felt terror, isolation, and deep sadness. So when my paternal Grandmother bought me a Batman T-shirt, it seemed like the perfect way to deal with my feelings of helplessness. I was completely convinced as I stood at the top of the stairs with my T-shirt on that I could fly and overcome adversity in spite of my life's circumstances. My sister had on her Robin T-shirt, and when I called her over to the top of the flight of stairs, she knew that it was going to end badly. She'd learned long ago, though, that to speak up was a big "no-no" in our house so she said nothing and proceeded to watch as I bumped and thumped my way down the flight of stairs. Needless to say, my hard head served me well even then and I came out of the ordeal relatively unharmed and still pretty certain of my invincibility.

My early school career was riddled with situations that would lay the groundwork for my future as an education super-HERO. Primary school was a safe and secure place where I could learn, play, and not worry about what type of drama might unfold at home. It was a welcome and important diversion from my home life. I was a classic "teacher's pet," and it just felt so good and safe that it didn't matter that the other kids didn't like me for being the pet; at that stage of my life, it was more important for me to feel safe than to have friends.

Unfortunately, on Christmas Day 1973, my life took a dramatic turn when my father died at the age of thirty-seven of a "heart attack." Truthfully, although he was a charismatic and loving man at times, he was a violent alcoholic who was bound by the circumstances of his youth. He died as a result of a fast life, poor diet, and numerous poor decisions. Shortly after he died, my mom finished her degree and got her first teaching job.

As I watched my mom's career unfold, I knew one thing for sure: I did not *ever* want to be a teacher! I listened in on the frequent calls to our home from angry parents, saw messages from principals who threatened her job, heard stories of students who were unruly, and carried boxes, after boxes, after boxes, back and forth each school year to a new classroom or school assignment. None of these entered my mind as something I would ever want to deal with or do for a career. I definitely wanted some *other* way out of difficult circumstances.

Shortly after my dad died, we moved to an area near the projects where my mom could afford a home on her annual teaching salary of $8,700. I encountered peers with a different skin color and attitude toward life, as well as a very different educational environment. The sign on the front of the new school said: "Who dares to teach, must never cease to learn." This quote from John Cotton Dana was a subtle message to me as I navigated these new challenges.

I learned *a lot* during those years in intermediate school. I learned to fight, to protect myself, to walk as quickly as possible, and to minimize any joy I might find because it would make me vulnerable to attack. I quickly hid my intellectual abilities, and as my resource reading teacher so eloquently informed my mom, I developed a tough exterior, or learned to be *hard*. That was the bad news. The good news was that the lessons I learned in those years were the foundation of my entire super-HERO mission and because of them I can better understand and support students struggling with life challenges better that many people. I also learned that every moment counts when a child is in trauma and needs adult support.

My peers in the new school had a love/hate relationship with me: The boys loved me and the girls hated me. Most days, the boys would follow me home while I was carrying my books and my cello and grab my privates, push me around, and make lewd comments all the four blocks home from school. Other days, the girls would follow me and hit me, push me, and make hateful comments to me while I was en route.

It was a very difficult and painful time in my life. I'd lost my father to death, my mother to escalating alcoholism, my sister to grief, and my waning innocence to my peers. Most disconcerting of all—and the foundation of my mission—is that in the small town where I lived, *nobody* ever stopped the car and pulled over to intervene in the 539 days I made that trek! The adults continued to drive by daily and seemed oblivious to the opportunity they had to be my super-HERO.

At last, someone *did* pull over. All I could think was, *finally*, some backup and relief. I was cussing, screaming, and yelling at the group of boys who had me circled and were grabbing me. Unfortunately, the driver was appalled by my language and chastised *me*, reminding me that a young lady doesn't talk that way and that I'd better start acting right. The boys laughed out loud, and I knew then that there would be no help on this journey of mine.

Because of my high standardized-test scores, I was placed in the high-track classes with affluent kids with whom I had very little in common with during my junior-high-school days. Being poor and without resources, my only option was to act angry, threatening, and rejecting. As I entered my teen years, my family situations escalated and I worked very hard to distance myself in any way possible from them. However, it was about this time that my Grandmother from the farm, who was struggling with poverty herself, bought the "right" for my name to be included in a publication called *Who's Who among American High School Students*. At the time, it didn't occur to me what a subtle message she was sending to my subconscious and future trajectory. Looking back, I'm sure she knew it might instill an ounce of confidence and pride in me, and she hoped that it might be enough to help me hold on and push for the next steps in my education as I fought through the alcoholism and violence at home.

The teachers I encountered during this time tried a variety of strategies to deal with me and my behavior and achievement. In her effort to help me live up to "my potential," Ms. Johnston, the social-studies teacher, woke me up in class and humiliated me by telling the class that if I wasn't so boy crazy, I might learn something. What she didn't realize was the police were often at my home until 4 or 5 a.m. dealing with my mother's series of drunken boyfriends and the domestic violence that was occurring. It was my "job" to protect her until the cops could get the man out and ensure that she was safe. The other teachers mostly seemed to disappear in the halls when the girls would corner me and threaten to beat me up. The woodshop teacher thought that if he threatened me with an F, it might motivate me to behave better in his class. Obviously, humiliation, threats, and invisibility weren't very effective tools to use with a kid who was struggling.

My junior-high and high-school experiences turned out to be a descent into hell. I found a group of friends at the skating rink and a group of friends at school. The kids at the skating rink had found their escape from home by going to the rink almost daily, and the kids I chose at school found their escape through alcohol and drugs. Over a period of time, the pursuit of the chemicals and their numbing effect on my hurt won out over my imagined career as a competitive skater.

Later in high school, several teachers tried other approaches to "help" me. They taught me a few new things about my future educational super-HERO journey. Ms. Bishop, the home-economics teacher, tried being "cool" and was my favorite at the time because she would let us come into class high or drunk, and we could cook and eat breakfast. Mr. Wagonner, my history teacher, tried being "kind" to me when I slept in his class; he would wake me up and ask me if I was okay. He even put me in charge of the Nuremburg mock trials to try to motivate me to participate in class. Although both of those teachers made efforts to build rapport with me, neither one of these strategies made the impact I needed to change the trajectory of my life.

Ironically, it was the school police officer who finally made that impact. He took me into his office, took apart some pills that kids were selling at school, and told me that even *he* didn't know what was in them. He spoke with truth and with heart; he didn't judge me but was honest with me. He told me that he was worried about me and that he was scared I was going to die if I kept doing the things I was doing. He had a crucial and critical conversation with me. Most adults shied away from that sort of thing, but this honest and direct approach was just what I needed to make me stop and consider my alternatives. He was a true super-HERO—and it only took **5 minutes** of his time to change my life.

Thank you Dave Senior! You taught me that everything matters for a kid who is desperately seeking a way out. I will never forget how that police officer made me feel. If you can do the same, you will unleash your inner super-HERO, and your actions may be the only way out for a student in difficult circumstances.

Your Mission: As you begin to fulfill your education super-HERO mission, think about Maslow's hierarchy of needs. Most of the research in learning shows that Maslow's hierarchy is still relevant and applicable to our 21st century classrooms. Today, our students and families are facing some, if not all, of the following barriers:

- *situational*—problems with employment, finances, child care, family, transportation, health, abuse
- *institutional*—program level or content, location, attendance/reentry policies
- *dispositional*—educational attitudes, self-efficacy, resilience, attribution of failure
- *emotional-relational*—social support and encouragement, caregiving

Instructional Implications

1. **What**—*What do I want to do? Which students are fighting the archenemy from this chapter?* Describe your mission around this issue:

   _____

   _____

   _____

2. **How**—*How will I get there and what do I need?* Review the super-HERO solutions/resources provided:
   - Children of Alcoholics: A Kit for Educators, Fourth Edition: 2001 http://www.nacoa.org/pdfs/EDkit_web_06.pdf
   - Social and Emotional Learning (SEL) and Student Benefits: Implications for the Safe Schools/Healthy Students Core Elements http://casel.org/wp-content/uploads/EDC_CASELSELResearch Brief.pdf

3. **Examine**—*Am I a super-HERO in this situation?* Evaluate your instructional and classroom-management behaviors to determine if they fit in with education super-HERO qualities:
   - **H:** Do my actions/behaviors *help*, not *hinder*?
   - **E:** Do my actions/behaviors *engage,* not *exclude*?
   - **R:** Do my actions/behaviors *resuscitate,* not *ruin*?
   - **O:** Do my actions/behaviors *overjoy,* not *obliterate*?

4. **Conclusion**—*How will I determine the results?* Gather data and anecdotal records to measure possible impact or modifications to make on attendance rates, behavior referrals, academic progress, parent involvement, etc.:

   _____

   _____

   _____

5. **Next Steps**—*What will I do if it didn't work?* List other like-minded individuals you can collaborate with who will encourage and support you on your journey:

   _____

   _____

   _____

6. **Celebrate**—*What went right this time?* Jot down your small successes here and document them in your own chapter at the back of the book:

   _____

   _____

   _____

Too often we underestimate the power of a touch, a smile, a kind word, a listening ear, an honest compliment, or the smallest act of caring, all of which have the potential to turn a life around.—Leo Buscaglia

CHAPTER 1

Welcome to the Jungle

Jermaine, Fighting Poverty

- **The Motto:** Guns N' Roses' "Welcome to the Jungle"—The lyrics describe how sometimes you have to learn to live like an "animal" to survive in difficult situations that could remind you of a jungle. My first teaching job felt like it was in a jungle at times.
- **The Sidekick:** Jermaine
- **The Archenemy:** Poverty
- **The Kryptonite:** Preconceived notions, limited vision, and lack of sensitivity and cultural awareness
- **The Super-HERO Lesson:** Things aren't always what they seem.
- **Social Emotional Learning Competency: Social awareness**

The first stop on my super-HERO mission was an inner-city elementary school in Opa-Locka, Florida. The statistics said that in 2004, Opa-Locka had the highest rate of violent crime for any city in the United States. The per capita income was approximately $15,000. A city today that is embroiled in corruption and scandals that permeate its structure and leaders. An Internet post from December 2011 described an apartment complex as follows:

> *"This is the worst place ever to live. To start, my neighbor is a stone cold drug addict and she prostitutes her two 13 year old daughters out to the entire complex to pay her rent. The management in the rent office sells bags of weed, cocaine, ex-pills and sex tapes. There is always gun shots like it's the fourth of July everyday. The lady down the hall sells food from her house and it has been reported that she has AIDS and she*

always be cutting herself from stress problems and leaking blood all over
the place!" (http://www.apartmentratings.com/rate/FL-Opa-Locka)

Many of our students were and still are living in these circumstances and even more treacherous ones. My hope in sharing this is to re-connect legislators and educators with the realities in our classrooms today in case they have forgotten or are unaware.

The students in the third-grade class had broken the teacher's leg in October during a fight in the classroom. I arrived for my first full-time teaching job in February after a series of substitutes refused to stay and finish the year. I was bright-eyed and excited to have my own classroom. *Batman* was a popular movie in 1990, and I had a friend help me build a library case from a Batman movie display. I bought a carpet for our reading area along with a lot of stickers and charts to set up my room and provide the students with incentives. I felt like I was truly on my way to education super-HERO status.

However, when I tried to quiet the class down so that I could talk, they got up and started running around, jumping off desks, screaming at me about being a "cracker," and asking one another, "Who does she think she is?" As I stood there feeling scared and helpless, the lyrics from the Guns N' Roses song, "Welcome to the Jungle" were playing so loudly in my head that all I could think to say to myself at the moment was, *"I quit! In college, this is not what they told me teaching was about, and I don't care about the $25,000 I just invested in a college degree. There is absolutely no way that I am dealing with this!"*

Fortunately, I stuck around and learned so many things that year. I learned about the effects of crack cocaine on children's physical, emotional, and intellectual development. The students struggled severely with impulse control and often burst out in fits of rage. I learned that teachers ate lunch in a lounge where cockroaches crawled across the table. The school was so old and dilapidated that there was no hope of containing outside influences. I learned that some students had homes with no floors when I did my home visits. I learned why kids wear coats in Florida—because the air-conditioning at school was something they didn't have at home. In 1990, not many educators were out there like I was trying to track down the parents to make sure that we could work together to help their child. Most of the people I knew refused to even drive in the area, let alone to go to the homes to learn more about their students and their lives. I learned that when the principal throws kids up against the wall and gets in their faces, they seem to calm down and "behave."

The aggressive behavior management seemed to be the only thing that the kids knew and would respond to.

Shortly after my arrival, the school board and a team of auditors came out to visit and determine the reasons why the school performed so poorly on yearly reviews. When they were done, the bureaucrats called us into a faculty meeting and proceeded to tell us that the school was a mess. They promised they would be back in a couple of months to help. Talk about *Waiting for Superman*; they never came back.

I quickly abandoned my "Boys and girls, we need to sit down" phase and started to find strategies to provide some structure and some rules to work with that would help meet the needs of the students. As part of our routine, we started watching the show *Reading Rainbow* every day to enhance their reading skills and for enjoyment. The kids made up their own song/rap that went along with the program, and I was in awe of the cool way they came together like a team each day when the show would come on.

As an addition to the show, I started my chart system with happy-face stickers to encourage them to complete homework. If they got a sticker for homework that day, I would give them two cookies to eat during *Reading Rainbow* time. It worked really well, and I felt like a super-HERO because the kids were doing homework and watching an educational program, and fighting had all but stopped in the classroom.

One kid, though, just wouldn't respond to the great strategies and interventions I had been implementing. He made jokes, laughed, and generally took the team off track whenever he could. A classic class clown. Then one day, he came in and had his homework! I was so excited. However, when he brought it to me, I was so disappointed. He seemed to be mocking me again and had turned it in on cardboard instead of paper. I think I told him that I would give him his sticker but not the cookies since he was still being "disrespectful" and didn't seem to value my system. He was upset but didn't say much else.

Not long after, I had an epiphany. After a couple of hours or days, maybe, I realized what I couldn't see before—the student, Jermaine, didn't have any paper to do his homework, so he had cut up a cereal box to turn in the work and get cookies!

My own preconceived notions, limited vision, and lack of sensitivity and cultural awareness blinded me to the reality and gravity of the situation that this young boy was living in. His innovation, determination, and resiliency astounded and impressed me so much that I almost started shouting from the rooftops about how pushing through your circumstances, whatever they are, makes you a *true hero*!

Thank you, Jermaine! I have used your story so many times in my work to make a point to apathetic students and even to try to jolt a teacher or two to wake up and see things they are missing. You were a huge part of my initial learning process and I truly hope that you were able to move onward and upward in your journey.

Your Mission: Reflect on how students in poverty bring many gifts to your classroom and find ways to teach them how to celebrate their gifts while they learn to navigate the rules of the middle class work and school environments they encounter.

Instructional Implications

1. **What**—*What do I want to do? Which students are fighting the same archenemy from this chapter?* Describe your mission around this issue:

    _____

    _____

    _____

2. **How**—*How will I get there and what do I need?* Review the super-HERO solutions/resources provided:
    - *A Framework for Understanding Poverty* by Ruby Payne
    - *Star Teachers of Children in Poverty* by Martin Haberman
    - *Teaching with Poverty in Mind: What Being Poor Does to Kids' Brains and What Schools Can Do about It* by Eric Jensen
    - *Resilience and Vulnerability: Adaptation in the Context of Childhood Adversities*, Chapter 11, "Poverty and Early Childhood Adjustment" by Suniya S. Luthar

3. **Examine**—Evaluate your instructional and classroom management behaviors to determine if they fit in with education super-HERO qualities:
    - **H:** Do your actions/behaviors *help*, not *hinder*?
    - **E:** Do your actions/behaviors *engage*, not *exclude*?
    - **R:** Do your actions/behaviors *resuscitate*, not *ruin*?
    - **O:** Do your actions/behaviors *overjoy*, not *obliterate*?

4. **Conclusion**—*How will I determine the results?* Gather data and anecdotal records to measure possible impact or determine modifications to make on attendance rates, behavior referrals, academic progress, parent involvement, etc.:

_____

_____

_____

5. **Next Steps**—*What will I do if it doesn't work?* List other like-minded individuals to collaborate with who will encourage and support you on your journey:

_____

_____

_____

6. **Celebrate**—*What went right this time?* Jot down your small successes here and document them in your own chapter at the back of the book.

_____

_____

_____

We know a good teacher can increase the lifetime income of a classroom by over $250,000. A great teacher can offer an escape from poverty to the child who dreams beyond his circumstance. Every person in this chamber can point to a teacher who changed the trajectory of their lives. ... Teachers matter.—President Barack Obama, 2012 State of the Union Address

CHAPTER 2

"This Is My Brother Darryl, and This Is My Other Brother Darryl"

Terry, Fighting Illiteracy and Identity issues

- **The Motto:** This line from the TV show *Newhart*—"This is my brother Darryl, and this is my other brother Darryl: illustrates a point about identity issues in this chapter.
- **The Statistics:** "70 out of 100 people in the world cannot read... if you can read then you are the luckiest out of 2 million people in the world that cannot." — Call Bain
- **The Sidekick:** Terry
- **The Archenemy:** Illiteracy
- **The Kryptonite:** Poverty, parental limitations, assumptions, lack of data/knowledgeable instruction/materials, and sometimes lack of patience
- **The Super-HERO Lesson:** Anything is possible, and probable, if you try!
- **Social Emotional Learning Competency: Responsible decision making**

In college, I majored in psychology and addictions treatment and quickly realized after my internship in a treatment center, that the low pay and the dysfunctional environment weren't a good fit for me. I decided to stay in school another year and major in education. I honestly wasn't sure about the profession. I just knew I wanted to help people and that the pay in education was better than in treatment centers.

My college had some great education professors, and my work in my reading course was with the text, *Becoming a Nation at Risk: The Report on the Commission on Reading.* Even in 1985, this book clearly highlighted two key points: (1) the knowledge is now available to make worthwhile improvements in reading throughout the United States, and (2) if the practices seen in the classrooms of the best teachers in the best schools could be introduced everywhere, improvement in reading would be dramatic. Something about that information solidified my suspicion that a teacher's strategic and intentional behaviors could have a tremendous impact on student behavior and learning. As we still struggle to level the playing field for all students, I continue to fight in a variety of venues to remind everyone that we have the knowledge and skills to change things, and for our students, we must embrace the schools who are getting it done right!

As part of my induction process, I encountered numerous issues in the urban, inner-city school where my career began. The school had very little, if any, supplies and the students had not been exposed to hands-on instruction or project based learning. I had to buy my own copy paper, classroom materials, and books. The students didn't know how to use glue sticks, so I had to use the industrial-sized container of paste for us to make a grammar flower of adjectives. I had been taught to do hands-on learning projects throughout my college career and I was completely baffled how the students were unable to glue the petals to the flowers with adjectives we had labeled. I was impatient and frustrated. I thought at first that they were just being difficult, but I finally realized that no one had ever done anything except worksheet activities with them, and this truly was a novelty for them.

Most of the students were over-age, underfed, and had few, if any, academic skills. So, they were desperately in need of a highly qualified and experienced teacher. Unfortunately, they were like most urban school kids and got a teacher who was completely clueless when it came to setting up small reading groups for instruction. I just tried to estimate what the students were capable of and tried to group them from there. I had some who seemed to be able to read, some who were having a hard time, and several who were nonreaders. We didn't use data or standardized testing much in 1990 and it truly was a "spray and pray" kind of mentality where you just tried to teach hard and fast and hope that the students learn something.

The nonreaders group was comprised of three young boys with a variety of demeanors: Mascott was the silly one (yes, that was his real name), Marcus was the quiet one, and Terry was the big one who was "angry." As I started my work with them, Marcus and Mascott seemed to progress, but Terry was stuck. I asked him if we could work together separately from the group, maybe like before and after school. After a few minutes, he said he wasn't sure, but that he might. He decided the next week to stay after school and give it a try. When we started our work, I told him that we should set a goal and that he should let me know what kind of surprise to get when he met his goal.

Terry looked me dead in the eye and asked me, "What's a surprise?" I was so shocked and sad that he didn't know what a surprise was, but I proceeded to tell him it was like a prize he could win for learning to read a number of word cards. He said "Oh!" and when I saw that he understood, I asked him what he would like his surprise to be for learning his first 30 words. He said he really didn't know what he wanted, and after a while he said he thought he would like to have some crayons.

You can imagine how I went right out and bought the biggest box of crayons I could find: the 64 box with the sharpener in it and everything. Terry came after school several times that week, and his twin brother came to wait for him to finish. Terry introduced me to his twin, whose name was also Terry. They were identical twins, ten years old, both nonreaders, both held back twice to still be in the third grade. I was so hurt that they didn't even get to have a name and identity of their own!

These boys had been failed by the adults around them for ten years, and I wanted to do everything I could to unleash my inner super-HERO and intervene in any way that I could. Terry worked hard and earned the surprise after a week of study. When I presented his box of crayons to him, he smiled and sat down quietly. Later that day, we were working on a math sheet that needed coloring. When it was time to color, the tears almost rolled down my face when Terry got up and walked around the room sharing his crayons with all the students in the class.

Thank you, Terry! I was so proud of your efforts and your kindness in sharing your materials. I never forgot that lesson and tried to honor your work with all of my future students by providing as many materials as I could and working hard to uncover my assumptions and expectations.

Your Mission: Spend some quiet time with yourself and think of all of the preconceived notions you have about what your students *should* know and what they *should* be getting at home. Often students hide the true depth of the things that are lacking at home. Although we can't afford to buy them so many of the things they deserve, the time you spend one-on-one just reaching out to a student could help you uncover one thing you could provide him with besides your time and your love and, most importantly, your respect.

Instructional Implications

1. **What**—*What do I want to do? Which students are fighting the archenemy from this chapter?* Describe your mission around this issue:

   _____

   _____

   _____

2. **How**—*How will I get there and what do I need?* Review the super-HERO solutions/resources provided:
   - Florida Center for Reading Research (fcrr.org): A comprehensive site that includes information, center activities, research, and best practices for all readers.

- *Becoming a Nation of Readers: The Report of the Commission on Reading,* The National Academy of Education, The National Institute of Education, The Center for the Study of Reading

3. **Examine**—*Am I a super-HERO in this situation?* Evaluate your instructional and classroom-management behaviors to determine if they fit in with education super-HERO qualities:
   - **H:** Do your actions/behaviors *help*, not *hinder?*
   - **E:** Do your actions/behaviors *engage*, not *exclude?*
   - **R:** Do your actions/behaviors *resuscitate*, not *ruin?*
   - **O:** Do your actions/behaviors *overjoy*, not *obliterate?*

4. **Conclusion**—*How will I determine the results?* Gather data and anecdotal records to measure possible impact or modifications to make on attendance rates, behavior referrals, academic progress, parent involvement, etc.:

   _____

   _____

   _____

5. **Next Steps**—*What will I do if it didn't work?* List other like-minded individuals to collaborate with who will encourage and support you on your journey:

   _____

   _____

   _____

6. **Celebrate**—*What went right this time?* Jot down your small successes here and document them in your own chapter at the back of the book.

   _____

   _____

   _____

Literacy is not a luxury, it is a right and a responsibility. If our world is to meet the challenges of the twenty-first century we must harness the energy and creativity of all our citizens.
—*President Clinton on International Literacy Day, September 8, 1994*

CHAPTER 3

Redneck Girl

Laura, Fighting lack of Family Resources

- **The Motto:** The Bellamy Brothers' "Redneck Girl" lyrics describe how a country girl plays her heart when she's down on her luck. This young lady and her family taught me numerous lessons about using your heart and loving others.
- **The Sidekick:** Laura
- **The Archenemy:** Lack of family resources
- **The Kryptonite:** Narrow-mindedness, assumptions
- **The super-HERO Lesson:** Use your heart to find like-minded collaborators in all kinds of places. Stay open and network for all your kids.
- **Social Emotional Learning Competency: Social Awareness**

As I got some years of teaching practice under my belt, I got the "privilege" of being the dropout-prevention teacher in the mainstream schools where I worked. I was so mad; it seemed like I was being punished for teaching the way that you're supposed to—by doing centers, projects, and playing kickball with my students. Turns out, like most things, it was a blessing in disguise.

A brand-new school was opening near my home, and they had an opening for a dropout-prevention teacher for a grade four/five combination class. I put my resume together and put my best foot forward. The guidance counselor who interviewed me thought that my psychology background and creative activities would be a great opportunity for the students, but she really liked the idea of the student-run restaurant that I had implemented at my last school. The students were in charge of planning, preparing, and serving meals to the extended community and parents in the classroom setting. It was a powerful initiative and created real-world, relevant learning long before that conversation made it to the education legislation.

After the first day of school that year, Laura and her mom sent me a thank-you card. Laura was so happy about having me for a teacher, and they were both excited about the activities that I had outlined for the year. I had never gotten much acknowledgement or thanks for doing the work I did, and especially not in the first days of school! Working in an affluent community was a new and refreshing opportunity for me. I had a small class, materials to use, parent support, and a brand-new team of teachers to work with. What I didn't know was that hurt, pain, dysfunction, and disappointment were still present in a community with more money—they just looked different.

Don't get me wrong; this time, there weren't knives and guns on the playground, none of my students were hungry. Our portable site had challenges, but it was clean and user-friendly. My vision for that year was a bit limited. I really had no idea how I was going to teach fourth- and fifth-grade material to students who had been placed in my classroom because of low test scores, behavior issues, or teacher recommendations. I knew that I wanted to continue on the path to find out more about what the kids needed academically, emotionally, and socially and to provide them with opportunities to be successful. I had a whole child and wrap around services mentality before it became popular.

To find extra support and wrap around services, I really started to branch out of the classroom and into the community. Laura's mom had shared with me some of their painful experiences through violent divorce proceedings, and I wanted to find ways for her to deal with it. Family counseling was available and we were able to work together to get them plugged in to that service from our school district for free. Later that year, we did a lot of creative projects and activities: we danced to "Redneck Girl" at the senior center for Valentine's Day, did our first student-run restaurant, had class meetings, and most importantly, went on a field trip to a community organization called Project Stable.

Project Stable was a nonprofit that took in animals in a farm setting and used 4-H curriculum and other tools to provide at-risk children some time with at-risk animals. Sandy McCartney, the founder, was a wonderful lady, and Laura took to her and her mission wholeheartedly. She started going to the ranch once a week after school and progressed to many days per week over time. Laura became enveloped in her work at the ranch, and after six or seven years of time there, she even got her own horse and got heavily involved in showing and performing. She stayed in touch with me over the years and today I connect with her and her mom on Facebook and watch as Laura supports and raises two incredible and beautiful sons. Sometimes our super-HERO work with kids is simply connecting them with resources for their time outside of school.

Thank you, Laura! It was an honor to walk beside you during the time we spent together and to learn so much about kindness and caring through our interactions. I have continued to pull in every community resource I can think of with my students over my career thanks to your success with Project Stable.

Your Mission: Look through your local weekly flyers and community news offerings to find two potential resources to contact for your students and their families. Reach out to them and start a partnership to better meet the needs of your kids.

Instructional Implications

1. **What**—*What do I want to do? Which students are fighting the archenemy from this chapter?* Describe your mission around this issue:

   _____

   _____

   _____

2. **How**—*How will I get there and what do I need?* Review the super-HERO solutions/resources provided:
   - National Dropout Prevention Center
     http://www.dropoutprevention.org/effective-strategies/school-community-collaboration
   - Communities in Schools
     http://www.communitiesinschools.org/about/
   - Center for American Progress
     http://www.americanprogress.org/wp-content/uploads/issues/2011/03/pdf/wraparound_services.pdf

3. **Examine**—*Am I a super-HERO in this situation?* Evaluate your instructional and classroom-management behaviors to determine if they fit in with education super-HERO qualities:
   - **H:** Do your actions/behaviors *help*, not *hinder*?
   - **E:** Do your actions/behaviors *engage*, not *exclude*?
   - **R:** Do your actions/behaviors *resuscitate*, not *ruin*?
   - **O:** Do your actions/behaviors *overjoy*, not *obliterate*?

4. **Conclusion**—*How will I determine the results?* Gather data and anecdotal records to measure possible impact or modifications to make on attendance rates, behavior referrals, academic progress, parent involvement, etc.:

   _____

   _____

   _____

5. **Next Steps**—*What will I do if it didn't work?* List other like-minded individuals to collaborate with who will encourage and support you on your journey:

_____

_____

_____

6. **Celebrate**—*What went right this time?* Jot down your small successes here and document them in your own chapter at the back of the book:

_____

_____

_____

Communities can provide schools with a context and environment that can either complement and reinforce the values, culture, and learning the schools provide for their students or negate everything the schools strive to accomplish. Communities also can furnish schools—and the students in them—with crucial financial support systems as well as the social and cultural values necessary for success and survival in contemporary society. Finally, communities have the potential to extend a variety of opportunities to students and to their families—social, cultural, and vocational.

—"The Importance of School and Community Collaboration"
Leaders for Tomorrow's Schools (http://www.michigan.gov/documents/
The_Importance_of_School_and_Community_Collaboration_156613_7.pdf)

CHAPTER 4

Drumming Is My Madness

Matt, Fighting ADD

- **The Motto:** Ringo Starr's "Drumming Is My Madness"—these lyrics describe how drumming can be maddening, pleasurable, business-oriented, and make someone very happy!
- **The Sidekick:** Matt
- **The Archenemy:** Attention deficit disorder
- **The Kryptonite:** Political correctness, lack of knowledge
- **The Super-HERO Lesson:** Sometimes you have to be willing to say the *wrong* thing to get the *right* results.
- **Social Emotional Learning Competency: Responsible decision making**

Matt was one of the many students I have encountered who had trouble concentrating, sitting still, finishing assignments, and organizing materials. Not only did he like to drum on the table most of the time I was talking, but he also felt a need to shout out during most of my instruction. He came to my fifth-grade dropout-prevention class in need of support, guidance, and most importantly, honesty.

What is Attention-Deficit Disorder?

ADD is officially called Attention-Deficit/Hyperactivity Disorder, or AD/HD (American Psychiatric Association, 1994), although most lay people, and even some professionals, still call it ADD or A.D.D. or ADHD. The name has changed as a result of scientific advances and field studies with students. ADHD is now divided into three subtypes, according to the main features associated with the diagnosis: inattentiveness, impulsivity, and hyperactivity.

Inattention

A child with ADHD is usually described as having a short attention span and as being distractible.

Symptoms of inattention, as listed in the DSM-IV, are:

- often fails to give close attention to details or makes careless mistakes in schoolwork, work, or other activities;
- often has difficulty sustaining attention in tasks or play activities;
- often does not seem to listen when spoken to directly;
- often does not follow through on instructions and fails to finish schoolwork, chores, or duties in the workplace (not due to oppositional behavior or failure to understand instructions);
- often has difficulty organizing tasks and activities;
- often avoids, dislikes, or is reluctant to engage in tasks that require sustained mental effort (such as schoolwork or homework);
- often loses things necessary for tasks or activities (e.g., toys, school assignments, pencils, books, or tools);

Hyperactivity

Excessive activity is the most visible sign of AD/HD. The hyperactive youth is generally described as "always on the go" or "motor driven."

Impulsivity

The impulsivity children exhibit is often to speak out of turn, interrupt others, and engage in what looks like risk-taking behavior. The child may run across the street without looking or climb to the top of very tall trees. Although such behavior is risky, the child is not really a risk-taker but, rather, a child who has great difficulty controlling impulse. Often, the child is surprised to discover that he or she has gotten into a dangerous situation and has no idea of how to get out of it.

This conversation is often highly charged and driven by emotional reactions. The school system has become very cautious in terms of what phrases a teacher may use when speaking with parents around this topic. The prescribed and politically correct way to let a parent know about this type of situation is to say, "I have "attentional" concerns about Matt." When I met with Matt's mom, she began to cry and share her frustration at not knowing what was wrong with him and what she could do to help. It appeared that the teachers that Matt and his mom had encountered along his educational career had avoided the topic out of fear of repercussions of being fired or sued for discussing the issue.

His mom knew Matt was smart, but she also seemed to recognize that he just couldn't stay focused. She'd tried many things over the years, but his learning and skill set had been impeded by his "attentional concerns." As we met and talked, I spoke the unspeakable: I asked her if she knew about ADD and if she had a physician who could check to see if this could be the problem. She said she had suspected it but since no one ever mentioned it, she hesitated to bring it up. We worked together with the school and the guidance counselor, and we found a great psychologist to support and assist Matt.

As we collaborated as a team, Matt began to improve, using a four-pronged approach to treating his ADD. Counseling, diet, exercise, and medication were the strategic interventions we used. We targeted his work and behaviors with a daily note system and continued to try to work on his study and organizational skills, which were both significantly impacted.

With this assistance, Matt's skill set increased and his on-task behavior skyrocketed. It came at a critical juncture, as Matt was in fifth grade and would soon be entering the large middle-school setting where he could have easily gotten lost.

Years later, I had lost touch with Matt and his mom but as I sat in the bench at a church I was visiting, I looked up to see Matt *drumming* in the band. He was happy and had made the transition to adulthood successfully thanks to our early interventions.

Thank you, Matt! Your courage and wisdom to work on issues beyond your control inspired me to do the same when I later faced issues that were similar to yours. I am so proud to know that your efforts paid off along your journey!

Your Mission: Step outside your comfort zone to try to encourage parents to seek out experts to help their child with attention and other chemically related issues. Research and reflect on all the different treatment modalities and how they can work together to assist a struggling student: diet, exercise, therapy, and medication.

Instructional Implications

1. **What**—*What do I want to do? Which students are fighting the archenemy from this chapter?* Describe your mission around this issue:

   _____

   _____

   _____

2. **How**—*How will I get there and what do I need?* Review the super-HERO solutions/resources provided:
   * *Right-Brained Children in a Left Brained World* by Jeffrey Freed and Laurie Parsons
   * *Driven to Distraction* by Edward M. Hallowell and John J. Ratey

- A.D.D. Coaching Group
  http://www.addcoachinggroup.com/index.htm

3. **Examine**—*Am I a super-HERO in this situation?* Evaluate your instructional and classroom-management behaviors to determine if they fit in with education super-HERO qualities:
   - **H:** Do my actions/behaviors *help*, not *hinder*?
   - **E:** Do my actions/behaviors *engage*, not *exclude*?
   - **R:** Do my actions/behaviors *resuscitate*, not *ruin*?
   - **O:** Do my actions/behaviors *overjoy*, not *obliterate*?

4. **Conclusion**—*How will I determine the results?* Gather data and anecdotal records to measure possible impact or modifications to make on attendance rates, behavior referrals, academic progress, parent involvement, etc.:

   _____

   _____

   _____

5. **Next Steps**—*What will I do if it didn't work?* List other like-minded individuals to collaborate with who will encourage and support you on your journey:

   _____

   _____

   _____

6. **6. Celebrate**—*What went right this time?* Jot down your small successes here and document them in your own chapter at the back of the book:

   _____

   _____

   _____

More and more, the concept of ADD as a disorder is being qualified by inclusion of a string of positive qualities—such as creativity, high intelligence, ability to do many things at once, an aptitude for small business entrepreneurship, and a powerful intuitive sense.—
Susan Burgess, from Think Fast! The ADD Experience

CHAPTER 5

Lean on Me

Christian, Fighting the Streets

- **The Motto:** Bill Withers' "Lean on Me"—these lyrics remind me that no matter what, we all need someone to lean on. The student sidekick, Christian chose them for his chapter.
- **The Sidekick:** Christian
- **The Archenemy:** The streets
- **The Kryptonite:** Family history and violence, criminal justice system
- **The Super-HERO Lesson:** You never know how much your presence means to a struggling youth.
- **Social Emotional Learning Competency: Responsible decision making**

According to a 2009 survey called "Children's Exposure to Violence: A Comprehensive National Survey" (http://www.unh.edu/ccrc/pdf/DOJ-NatSCEV-bulletin.pdf):

> "Most of our society's children are exposed to violence in their daily lives. More than 60 percent of the children surveyed were exposed to violence within the past year, either directly or indirectly (i.e., as a witness to a violent act; by learning of a violent act against a family member, neighbor, or close friend; or from a threat against their home or school) ... Nearly one-half of the children and adolescents surveyed (46.3 percent) were assaulted at least once in the past year, and more than 1 in 10 (10.2 percent) were injured in an assault; 1 in 4 (24.6 percent) were victims of robbery, vandalism, or theft; 1

in 10 (10.2 percent) suffered from child maltreatment (including physical and emotional abuse, neglect, or a family abduction); and 1 in 16 (6.1 percent) were victimized sexually. More than 1 in 4 (25.3 percent) witnessed a violent act." This doesn't include the video games and social media culture of violence exposure. The students we serve are desensitized to violence causing the social emotional learning competencies being proposed to become even more critical for all of us to learn and embrace.

Christian was one of those children. His preschool records were full of accounts of him being "bad" and fighting. It's almost impossible to believe that anyone could consider a child at that age as being bad and not try to look below the surface to see what was making this child fight at such a young age. Unfortunately, most days when I walk in to the kindergarten and grade 1 classrooms where I provide instructional coaching, it happens often and it breaks my heart for adults to confront, attack, and humiliate little children who are more than likely struggling with similar issues to Christian.

He told me that his mom was in a gang and his dad was in jail, so they gave him and his older brother to their Grandpa to raise. Grandpa was an older Cuban immigrant in Miami who was just getting by on minimum-wage jobs. Still, he would provide a safer and more secure environment for the four- and five-year-old boys.

Christian and his brother had more battles to fight, as they had to learn a new home system and a new school system. They were very close and probably clung to each other to find a sense of love and belonging. Over time, just the two of them wasn't enough, and Christian's older brother got involved with the neighborhood gangs. Christian was not about to be left out and was also initiated at a very young age into a gang that would rob and steal to get extra money for things they wanted. His elementary years and early high-school years were riddled with "charges he caught," time in programs and facilities, and suspensions from different schools.

I met Christian the first day I worked in a credit recovery/alternative education high school. The students were ages sixteen to twenty-one and had not been successful in traditional education settings. The curriculum was an online course format for students to work independently through their high-school courses with minimal teacher support. I was serving as the reading coach and was there to support struggling readers and to monitor a separate online reading program. I was excited and truly looked forward to recognizing the numerous students who were still stuck reading on a third-, fourth, or fifth-grade level for their hard work and progress that could ultimately lead to a diploma. Many of the students had been in and out of the court system for various offenses, including drugs, robbery, and gang-related activities.

When I met Christian that first day, I could tell that he had been in some type of facility for a long period of time because of his demeanor and his conversation with me. He kept quiet, kept his head down, and said "yes ma'am" quite a bit. I encouraged him and all the other students to get started in the online reading program so that we could increase their scores, pass the state tests, and earn high-school elective credits. As I checked in with students as they started the program, Christian quietly told me that he had already passed the FCAT and that he didn't think he needed to do the reading program. As we talked, I asked him if he had his scores and tried to determine how many credits he would need to graduate. He said that all the records were in the program where he was and that they were supposed to be sending it all to this current school.

During the next several months, I had him work with the front office numerous times to try to get his records sent to the school so that I could confirm that he had actually passed the state test and met that graduation requirement. Day by day, we talked a bit more, and I reverted back to my method of having students do jobs and take ownership of different aspects of the school. I asked Christian to become my Reading Plus student advocate and told him that I needed a PowerPoint presentation designed and work done over the weekend if he was interested. He agreed, and I am certain that on some level he was shocked when I handed him my personal laptop in a bag to take home over the weekend. It had probably been so long since someone had trusted him and believed in him that he might have been in shock! I knew that he would protect and take care of the laptop and that he would do a great job of working with students in the Reading Plus program.

My morning routine each day was to watch the students when they came through the metal detectors and arrive for class. I always put up motivation quotes, contests, or other items to encourage the students as they entered the building. I knew it was critical to help them find ways to shift their energy and be ready to learn. Their weekends were inevitably filled with stress, sadness, and struggle. My songs, hugs, and silly comments were the reason I got up every morning. I knew the kids needed me and I knew that I made a difference for the kids. Monday came, and when Christian came through the metal detectors with the laptop, the security guard went wild asking him where he got the laptop and telling him that he wasn't allowed to have it. I intervened immediately and winked at Christian when I told the guard that it was *my* laptop and that Christian took it home to help me. When the guard later warned me about "these" kids, I just chalked it up to another person who didn't get me or get kids—even though I was very mad at him for working in a place where he was more of a detriment than an asset to "my" kids. Some of the adults in the urban schools where I have worked have permeated the school culture and climate with negative thoughts, feelings, behaviors, and comments about the kids.

Christian took a while to get some of the technical glitches out, but we kept working together to build a solid presentation and work up to him delivering the content. As we got closer, I learned that as a 16 year-old, he had sixteen charges and four felonies, had been in two programs, and was hoping that he could steer his way clear of all of it when he turned 18 and move on to a career as an auto mechanic.

I saw that he was able to teach himself pre-calculus online and that he was reading at the college level in Reading Plus, and I told him there was *no way* that he should be a car mechanic! He was bright and could have any career he wanted and I felt strongly that he was settling for this because he didn't believe he had any other options. He would have made a fantastic attorney, but his criminal record prohibited him from pursuing that career. He liked and was good at engineering, and we spent a lot of time researching grants, visiting a work and college program for ex-offenders, collaborating with other agencies and probation officers, and just tried to keep things moving in a positive direction. In hindsight, I wonder if my naïve optimism was a detriment in the overall course of his life.

Each time we tried a new route, another obstacle was thrown in the way. He couldn't file his FAFSA papers until he got his Grandpa's tax returns. Grandpa didn't trust that Christian would do the right thing so he wouldn't help. I wrote a note and subsequently tried to go to the house to meet him to explain and show him what we were trying to do. I met the Grandma instead, and she proceeded to let me know that Christian was a bad kid and that I shouldn't trust him. I was heartbroken for him. He had made so many mistakes and was not in an environment that would support change.

Next came the attempts to get to job interviews and programs. He needed a bus pass to get to the sites that were far from his house, but he didn't have the money. I took him a couple of times but still had to maintain some type of boundaries and had to try to get him to be resourceful and develop a large new network of support. It was often an exercise in futility.

Graduation day came, and I was able to get the school to pay for his cap and gown fee so that he could walk on the stage. He was the first one to graduate from his family, and he hoped that his Grandma and Grandpa could make it. Grandpa worked part-time in a grocery store, and neither of the two of them attended. I called Christian about an hour prior to graduation time, and he told me that he was probably going to be late as he had to ride the city bus to get to the ceremony since nobody could give him a ride. I told him to stay put and got to his location as fast as I could. A friend of his who was pregnant also attended the ceremony, and she and I screamed his name as loud as we could when he got his diploma. Afterward, I took them to a Chinese buffet to celebrate and took them home. What a great day!

We tried several different times to get his college set up, but there seemed to be hurdle after hurdle after hurdle. In the meantime, his girlfriend became pregnant, and he was uncertain of how he could find a way to provide for her and their child. Work applications all asked for felony reporting, and he hadn't had much luck with some of the programs. That summer, an opportunity came through with a nonprofit group, Opportunities Industrialization Centers of South Florida (OIC-SFL), and Christian worked the front desk and translated for immigrants needing social services. He got high ratings, got paid, and did an awesome job for the eight weeks that he was allowed to work. As things wound down, the baby was born and life just kept getting harder.

He finally turned 18 and was almost "born again" in the sense that he could have a clear record and a clear future. I was so proud and excited for him! We met up one morning for breakfast and had fun taking pictures of him and his baby daughter and sharing a lot of positive thoughts and future plans. I reached out via text and phone a couple times over the next month but didn't hear back from him. I tried to dismiss it that he was just busy and that we would talk again soon.

One day when I was researching court records for a traffic ticket, and on a whim I also searched for records under his name, and was stupefied to find the following:

Charge Detail								
Select Charge	Charge	Citation/ NTA Number	Status	Offense Date	Statute	Description	Filed On	Filed By
O	1		OPEN	03/08/2012		Possess Cannabis/20 Grams Or Less		

I was so sad and hurt, and I called him immediately. He claimed the same thing all kids do—it would be dropped and everything would be okay. I was tough with him and told him that his daughter needed him and that he better get back with some programs and get himself in school. He promised he would, and I walked away with a grim hope that he could turn it around.

Several months later, when I was getting ready to pay my fine for the traffic ticket, I found that he now had incurred a first-degree felony with five separate charges of fleeing, battery of a law-enforcement officer, and other items. When I saw it, I couldn't even call him. I just texted him and asked him what happened. His response: "Charges will get dropped dey made a false police report."

I couldn't even argue or respond. So many days I wonder if *anything* I have done makes a difference in the trajectory of a kid's life, and it brings tears, hurt, and disappointment. It is a very hard lesson for me to learn and was a big part of telling my student stories to you so that you could know that you are not alone and to not give up.

Christian read the draft of the book and his chapter. He told me that *kids* should read it, and I responded with, "Are you crazy? Some of you died, reoffended, etc. *Why* should kids read it?" He said the same thing I say to you: "So they will know that they are not alone." Christian is in prison now and I don't know when, or if, he will get out. Although it is heartbreaking to me, I truly want to believe that having me to "lean on" during his senior year made his immediate and future life better.

Thank you Christian! Your willingness to trust me and allow me to walk beside you in your struggles made me wiser and helped me to see that this book is for students too. I hope that I was able to plant the seeds for your future success.

Your Mission: Continue to find other like-minded people in the trenches and get the support, encouragement, and love you need to continue to fight the good fight and find your own inner peace.

Instructional Implications

1. **What**—*What do I want to do? Which students are fighting the archenemy from this chapter?* Describe your mission around this issue:

   _____

   _____

   _____

2. **How**—*How will I get there and what do I need?* Review the super-HERO solutions/resources provided:
   - "Responding to Gangs in the School Setting" http://www.nationalgangcenter.gov/Content/Documents/Bulletin-5.pdf: Helping students in gangs
   - Gang Resistance Education and Training Program http://www.great-online.org/

3. **Examine**—*Am I a super-HERO in this situation?* Evaluate your instructional and classroom-management behaviors to determine if they fit in with education super-HERO qualities:
   - **H:** Do your actions/behaviors *help*, not *hinder*?
   - **E:** Do your actions/behaviors *engage*, not *exclude*?
   - **R:** Do your actions/behaviors *resuscitate*, not *ruin*?
   - **O:** Do your actions/behaviors *overjoy*, not *obliterate*?

4. **Conclusion**—*How will I determine the results?* Gather data and anecdotal records to measure possible impact or modifications to make on attendance rates, behavior referrals, academic progress, parent involvement, etc.:

   _____

   _____

   _____

5. **Next Steps**—*What will I do if it didn't work?* List other like-minded individuals to collaborate with who will encourage and support you on your journey:

   _____

   _____

   _____

6. **Celebrate**—*What went right this time?* Jot down your small successes here and document them in your own chapter at the back of the book:

_____

_____

_____

"The perception that teachers care about their students is among the strongest predictors of student performance." Dweck, Walton, & Cohen, 2011

CHAPTER 6

Jacked Up

Danny, Fighting for "Bad kids"

- **The Motto:** A line from the movie *Talladega Nights*—"I'm gonna come at you like a spider monkey ... I'm all jacked up on Mountain Dew." Danny was one of those students who had more energy and issues than most and he had been labeled as a "bad kid."
- **The Sidekick:** Danny
- **The Archenemy:** Ineffective leadership styles and "old-fashioned" teachers
- **The Kryptonite:** Lack of knowledge, fear/bullying, self-righteousness
- **The Super-HERO Lesson:** Discern the message ... from the messenger!
- **Social Emotional Learning Competency: Self-management**

"Oh, just go in your room and look the other way ..."

This has become an all-too-familiar phrase during the span of my educational career. My peers and outside friends often told me to just go in my classroom and close the door to the issues or needs of the students who were in trouble and needed my help. This struggle for fighting injustices with integrity and somehow playing the game to keep a job happens in every industry at one time or another. However, for me, when a child's life can potentially hang in the outcome of how this type of situation plays out, there has been NO HESITATION on how to proceed. The audacity of the adults around me to become blind to the impact on kids is one of my biggest triggers and battles to fight. My job has been jeopardized many times and I have been labeled the "troublemaker" due to my refusal to look the other way. I am somehow blessed and cursed with the ability to see and believe that *everything* we do or don't do for a student can and does have an impact. Many of those educational leaders who labeled me left a lasting impression … of what *not* to do to in educational settings for students.

One principal in particular had such a profound impact that I have even gone back in subsequent years to thank her. It was pretty funny, actually; she thought I was thanking her for all of her help, but I was truly thanking her for being so incredibly *awful* to me and my students. My interactions with her ultimately pushed me to leave the public system and start my own successful tutoring company and, later, award-winning charter school!

Most, if not all, of my students brought a plethora of issues to the table when they came to my class. Danny was an overage boy who had blond hair, blue eyes, a football build, and a voice as loud as a stock trader on a very bad day. He brought more energy to the door at eight a.m. every morning than I might gather all day. Many times I would have to meet him at the door, speak quietly and calmly, pat him on the back, and tell him that when he could get himself calmed down some, he could enter the classroom. I tried many interventions to help Danny be successful: progress stickers, class-wide points, calls home, individual meetings, recess reduction, and as many things as I could think of to help him to avoid failing and to start behaving in class. When we sent out the first interim reports that year, Danny had earned mostly D and F grades because of his lack of follow-through, consistency, attention, and behaviors. His attention issues and lack of solid foundational academic skills were a tough barrier to penetrate.

We were required to turn the reports in to the principal prior to distribution, and after she viewed mine, she called me to her office. When I arrived, she, the guidance counselor, and the assistant principal were sitting in a line facing the chair that I was to sit in. It was a pretty intimidating setup for me to walk into, but I just sat down anyway because I didn't think there could be any type of problem. Boy, was I wrong!

The group of administrators asked why some of my students had low grades and I explained the situation to them. They knew that I was teaching drop-out prevention in a combination grade 4/5 class with little, if any, resources or support for the 18 students who had struggled before coming to my class. I shared that I had called home and put many positive and disciplinary consequences in place as well as many academic and instructional interventions and that is what the kids had *earned*. The principal then proceeded to tell me that I had not done my job and that I would change those grades whether the students earned them or not: I wouldn't earn tenure and I would be replaced if I didn't. I was shocked and stupefied. She also informed me that the interventions I had provided were not enough and that I must individualize systems for every student in the class who wasn't successful. She had not stepped foot into my classroom yet and she hadn't reviewed any of my lesson plans, interventions, differentiated work, or supported me in any fashion. I had done so much of the Response to Intervention work years before it became a part of the educational process and was baffled when other teachers seemed to find it difficult to implement.

Now, I felt that I had already done this, but I was still scared that I would lose my job and felt that I'd better try something. After I got done bawling and screaming, I tried to think about what else I could do. I ended up setting up an individual monitoring system for Danny that would have him track three specific behaviors to monitor and manage to increase his success. I sat down with Danny and his parents, and we came up with a chart and monitoring support system that looked something like this:

GOALS	5 MIN.	10 MIN.	15 MIN.	20 MIN.	25 MIN.	30 MIN.
Stay in seat						
Raise hand						
Finish work						
Hands/self						

Point rewards: 30 points by lunch: full recess, 20 points by lunch: ½ recess
Extra points can be saved for bonus reward: Show-n-Tell with snake-(This was the ultimate prize for Danny's choice and motivation)

It was a lot of extra work, but the chart put me ahead of the curve several years later when rubrics and positive behavioral supports came into fashion. Danny's behavior and grades improved, but I had to pray a lot that year and I earned every penny I got as I tried to help him and the other 17 students with individualized plans.

Thank you, Danny! My time with you that year taught me so much about how tough it is for some kids to internally monitor what is happening with them. You were one of the few students who forced *me* to speak quiet, stay calm, and be patient—incredibly important traits in my work!

In that time period in education, many administrators forgot to support and help teachers in order to help them grow professionally and teachers often felt hurt, bullied, alone, and scared. The bullying tactics that this principal used were not helpful or supportive for me to develop as an educator. Fortunately for Danny and the other students, I was able to take the lemons that they handed me and do my best to make lemonade from them.

Your Mission: Choose one student who needs individual behavior support and implement a system with the student's input to assist him or her in increasing positive and rewarding behavior.

Instructional Implications

1. **What**—*What do I want to do? Which students are fighting the archenemy from this chapter?* Describe your mission around this issue:

   _____

   _____

   _____

2. **How**—*How will I get there and what do I need?* Review the super-HERO solutions/resources provided:
   - Positive Behavioral Interventions and Supports
     http://www.pbis.org/
   - "Positive Behavior Support and Functional Behavioral Assessment for Educators"
     http://www.education.com/reference/article/positive-behavior-support-functional-behavioral/
   - "CHAMPS—Classwide Positive Behavior Support (PBS)"
     http://www.safeandcivilschools.com/services/classroom_management.php; CHAMPS behavioral system

3. **Examine**—*Am I a super-HERO in this situation?* Evaluate your instructional and classroom-management behaviors to determine if they fit in with education super-HERO qualities:
   - **H:** Do my actions/behaviors *help*, not *hinder*?

- **E:** Do my actions/behaviors *engage*, not *exclude*?
- **R:** Do my actions/behaviors *resuscitate*, not *ruin*?
- **O:** Do my actions/behaviors *overjoy*, not *obliterate*?

4. **Conclusion**—*How will I determine the results?* Gather data and anecdotal records to measure possible impact or modifications to make on attendance rates, behavior referrals, academic progress, parent involvement, etc.:

_____

_____

_____

5. **Next Steps**—*What will I do if it didn't work?* List other like-minded individuals to collaborate with who will encourage and support you on your journey:

_____

_____

_____

6. **Celebrate**—*What went right this time?* Jot down your small successes here and document them in your own chapter at the back of the book:

_____

_____

_____

People's behavior makes sense if you think about it in terms of their goals, needs, and motives.—Thomas Mann

CHAPTER 7

Who Ya Gonna Call?

Michael, Fighting Implementation issues

- **The Motto:** "Ghostbusters: Who ya gonna call?"—these lyrics ask that if something strange is going on and you can see it, who ya gonna call? This story illustrates this concept on both a figurative and literal level as school staff turned a blind eye and refused to call for help-even when a ghost presented itself in conversation.
- **The Sidekick:** Michael
- **The Archenemy:** Good intentions
- **The Kryptonite:** Apathetic staff, refusal to confront issues, mental illness
- **The Super-HERO Lesson:** Champion your students in every way you can!
- **Social Emotional Learning Competency: Relationship skills**

As I expanded my career to middle school, I continued to specialize in struggling learners but did it in one hour blocks in content areas of language arts and social studies instead of the day long setting of elementary school. While I was pregnant, I continued to teach and planned to work as long as I could before the due date. One day a young man was coming up the ramp to my portable classroom and I thought he might be a new janitor because he was tall, had tattoos on his arms, and had a rough face and build. It turns out, he was a new student named Terrance who was 14 years old in the 6th grade. He struggled to behave and when I tried to hold him accountable for his behavior, he told another teacher that he was going to kick me in the stomach and hurt me and my baby. When I expressed concern, the principal told me not to be so dramatic and that everything would be fine. It turned out that this young man had been in foster homes for most of his life, had recently broken a kid's arm, and was just coming out of a juvenile justice facility. I resigned for the first time in my career and was furious by the lack of caring, acknowledgment, and support I received on this issue from the principal. Especially since the teacher's union had just negotiated a contract item that teachers with just cause could have a student removed from their classroom.

The following school year after my son was born and a new principal was in place, I returned to the school. I agreed to set up and take on one of their new initiatives, the JET program. It was designed as an alternative to suspension for students who misbehaved and were to be suspended. If they met the program requirements: attendance, completion of work, counseling sessions, they could stay in school and avoid negative ramifications on their school records.

The program was housed in an offsite location in a trailer park that had a building to serve the students about 20 minutes from the home school. There were three other nearby schools who would send students to the site if needed but it was supervised by my home school and new principal. Besides not having materials or any close-by support, the facility was not in working condition. The ceiling had holes from a leaky roof, the phone lines and fax machine weren't connected yet, the bathrooms were in need of repair, and the protocols and processes for intake, instruction, and schedules were not in place. As with all my other educational adventures, I became resourceful and worked with the counselor to set up some structure and facilitate a climate and culture for learning and support for the students and families, even though there were an inordinate amount of problems.

Students who were suspended for habitual behaviors, disrespect, not performing, fighting, and drugs were some of the main customers who started to attend. Most of the kids had learning difficulties and were in need of multiple streams of support. We worked tirelessly to set up the building and gather materials. I wasn't there too long before things got very serious, very quickly.

One student, Michael, was a resident of the local trailer park and had a history of family problems and police and social-worker visits. Michael came to the JET program feisty and full of fury. He was on the small side and had several scars on his face from his dealings in the past. As I reached out to our guidance department to find out more about how to help him, the guidance director informed me that no one would go to the home anymore because of the vast numbers of pit bulls and threats of attack when social workers had gone out in the past. They decided to look the other way or turn their heads because it was difficult and challenging to support this young man and his family.

I wanted to help Michael, and after assessing his reading skills, I found out that he was unable to read beyond a basic first-grade level. I assigned one of the older high-school students who had been with us a couple of days to assist Michael in his sentence practice for phonics and spelling. They started with a sentence for the short sound of *a*.

1. I plan to kill the teacher.

Then, they moved to the short sound of *u*.

2. My brother has a gun.

As I walked around the room and monitored, I checked on the boys and stepped back when I saw what Michael had written. I wasn't exactly scared, but I did tell Michael that he couldn't write things like that down and that it would get him in a lot of trouble. Later on I realized that this could be a legitimate concern for me and the counselor. We were housed in an offsite facility with phone service that was working sometimes at best, and no support or security within fifteen to twenty-five minutes.

I faxed my assistant principal the work and called to explain that we needed to get Michael additional help and that we needed to put together a better safety and security plan. She promised to get back to me later that day. She didn't and I knew the district mandated a parent conference and/or contact to discuss the incident before any further discipline could be implemented. I wanted to follow the correct procedures and caught a break when Michael was absent the next day to wait for more information about how to deal with the situation. When I didn't hear back by the end of the second day, I did two things: called the principal in charge and called Michael's mom.

The principal told me he would deal with it. By the end of the day, he still hadn't contacted me so I felt that my only option was to e-mail the union and cc'd the principal to ask for help and guidance for my safety. The principal was quick to respond after that. He called and yelled, cursed, and threatened me for going beyond our "family," and he said that I was going to be called on the carpet for this. I stayed calm and simply told him that I would resign if my safety was in jeopardy and he wasn't going to support me.

The call to Michael's mom was another story. When I got her on the phone and tried to talk with her about coming in to meet with me and put together a plan for Michael's success, she apologized for his absence, but said they'd had a ghost in the house the night before and they had been awake dealing with it.

In my seven years of teaching, I had *never* heard anything so outlandish, and I was almost speechless. My goal was to help Michael, so without missing a beat, I told her that I understood and that it was good to work together as a family, but we needed to meet and set up a plan for him to come back and complete the JET program.

As you can imagine, neither meeting ever happened because due to the lack of school support and my safety concerns, I chose to resign my position at the end of that day. My friends at the school told me that Michael struggled through the rest of the year with the same types of issues, and it was simply a merry-go-round of him being in and out of suspension and eventually failing the 6th grade.

I wasn't sure what ever happened to Michael, but my experience with him taught me an important lesson learned: While there are many great initiatives, textbooks, technology purchases, and programs for students, most of them are not thought through, trained for, or even supported by the staff. Lack of buy-in and challenges come from not being able to take one issue at a time and put all the emotional, financial, and intellectual resources into getting things done right. The lack of understanding that doing things right *does* make a difference is often the biggest barrier.

Thank you, Michael! My experience and time with you framed my thinking to better serve students with quality initiatives in my future endeavors. I truly had hope that you landed somewhere safe and secure in your journey.

Update: As I was outside of a Dunkin Donuts recently, a student from that time period and I met up and caught up on what he had been doing in the last 15 years since he was in my class. He shared a lot of tales and I proceeded to tell him about this book. As we talked, I asked him about Michael and if he knew what happened to him. He did and he proceeded to tell me. Michael had struggled as I suspected he would, and as he and his girlfriend were arguing, he shot himself and took his own life. It broke my heart and re-affirmed my need to push through writing this book for the next student who needs help.

Your Mission: When designing programs, interventions, and support programs be sure to research best practices and try to find the best staff to implement the initiatives and support them.

Instructional Implications

1. **What**—*What do I want to do? Which students are fighting the archenemy from this chapter?* Describe your mission around this issue:

   _____

   _____

   _____

2. **How**—*How will I get there and what do I need?* Review the super-HERO solutions/resources provided:
   - "What Is RTI?"
     http://rtinetwork.org/learn/what/whatisrti
   - Effective Strategies for Dropout Prevention
     http://www.dropoutprevention.org/effective-strategies
   - National School Reform Faculty: Critical Conversations with staff
     http://www.nsrfharmony.org/faq.html

3. **Examine**—*Am I a super-HERO in this situation?* Evaluate your instructional and classroom-management behaviors to determine if they fit in with education super-HERO qualities:

   - **H:** Do my actions/behaviors *help*, not *hinder?*
   - **E:** Do my actions/behaviors *engage*, not *exclude?*
   - **R:** Do my actions/behaviors *resuscitate*, not *ruin?*
   - **O:** Do my actions/behaviors *overjoy*, not *obliterate?*

4. **Conclusion**—*How will I determine the results?* Gather data and anecdotal records to measure possible impact or modifications to make on attendance rates, behavior referrals, academic progress, parent involvement, etc.:

   _____

   _____

   _____

5. **Next Steps**—*What will I do if it didn't work?* List other like-minded individuals to collaborate with who will encourage and support you on your journey:

   _____

   _____

   _____

6. **Celebrate**—*What went right this time?* Jot down your small successes here and document them in your own chapter at the back of the book:

   _____

   _____

   _____

Every child deserves a champion—an adult who will never give up on them, who understands the power of connection and insists that they become the best that they can possibly be. --Rita F. Pierson

CHAPTER 8

Hey, Mr. DJ!

Alberto, Fighting Cultural and Age Gaps

- **The Motto:** Madonna's song "Music"—the lyrics in this song describe how music can be an equalizer for all age and gender groups and "make the people come together": the bourgeoisie and the rebel. Music was a relationship builder for me with this student.
- **The Sidekick:** Alberto
- **The Archenemy:** Special-education services and legislation that often times keeps students from getting what they need
- **The Kryptonite:** Family issues, addiction issues, lack of support, lack of training
- **Super-HERO Lesson:** Learn to trust your gut and never give up on fighting for kids!
- **Social Emotional Learning Competency: Self awareness**

Later in my career, as I interviewed for a consulting position, I was required to write a passage and standard test questions to accompany it. I thought I was pretty good at designing questions like the state assessment test, the FCAT, since I had gotten some stem sets along the way and had used them in my classes. My students and I worked together often to design test questions and distractors for a deeper understanding of our content. However, I had never written a passage before and thought that it might be tough for me.

As I began writing, it was pretty clear that I had been teaching struggling learners for a long time. My lower vocabulary, short and chunked information, and use of emotion and humor to engage my students were huge barriers to writing a passage on the 10th grade level. It turns out I knew very little about how to use the right kind of distracters and applications of those stems to guide student learning the way they needed for success as well. Many teachers were never properly trained in this area and I still worry often about the untrained teachers who are tasked with writing curriculum and aligning it with the standards.

I wrote the following story about a young man I had in my class who had struggled for a long time. I asked him to be my DJ during our activities several times, and he not only enjoyed it but tried to "save me" from the principal one day when she was about to enter our classroom while we were playing music as we worked on projects. He was very protective of those he cared about and was worried I would get in trouble. Here are the passage and rudimentary question sets:

Before it's too late

"What's up, Miss?" he exclaimed in a bellowing voice with a Hispanic accent as he crossed the threshold of the rundown, dilapidated portable to attend his intensive reading class. This would be the third time Alberto took the state examination, and as he recalled the results of past attempts in his mind, he was sure he knew what the result would be. It was bewildering to me that this young man had received some type of special education services but had been unsuccessful in all of his eleven years in formal education. How could he have gotten to this stage of life without being able to read successfully? Wasn't he being supported and helped?

The challenge for me as a teacher was the same every day: unravel all the discouragement and disillusionment students frequently felt while quickly diagnosing what each would need to be engaged, empowered, and encouraged for that particular day. I had been at this juncture with students numerous times and knew that if the kid would meet me halfway, Alberto could conquer anything.

In the gang-infested streets of the barrio, conquering anything educationally was a true road to success. It was obvious that countless numbers of students wanted to do well, but it would take an inordinate amount of encouragement, instruction, and support. When it came to passing the test, I felt strongly that if I taught hard enough, fast enough, and with enough emotion, success was a certainty.

After a lengthy day of high-powered instruction, the final class brought the most rambunctious set of students. As they entered like a herd of cattle, my initial thoughts were confirmed: the obnoxious behaviors they displayed cued me in quickly to the fact that their needs were immense, and my energy was waning. Convincing them was going to take everything I had.

The administration had assigned the novel *Killing Mr. Griffin* for the intensive reading class that year, and while the other teachers balked at the absurdity of the concept, I knew better. The thought of urban inner-city high-school youth reading a novel account of how students kidnapped and killed their English teacher hit a little too close to home for the other teachers, but I already had a deep appreciation and understanding of engagement and empowerment of students and had a pretty clear vision of the possibilities that the project might bring about. Entering the school each morning could bring about that feeling of fear in a teacher, but I never let those ludicrous thoughts discourage my zest.

I knew it was simple: continue to be honest with students, treat them fairly, firmly, and consistently, all while providing instruction that engaged and empowered them. In my mind, there was no better place in the world than in that classroom.

I switched gears and elaborated on an engaging idea to win them over. They would be read the novel and adapt it to a screenplay format. The entire concept appealed on multiple levels to the students, and they responded favorably. The enormity of it reenergized me as a teacher: I was "throwing the starfish back" one at a time. I reflected back on that story often, and it gave me tremendous comfort in the dark times from which I had recently emerged. Fighting cancer and having to leave the charter school I had founded was one of the hardest things I had ever encountered and it left me floundering and unsure of next steps. My mother's passing shortly after that started what I have now deemed, "the decade of disaster." But I continued to fight because when everyone else had given up on students, I knew that getting just one of them to success was worth all the effort it entailed. It was also clear that even though it seemed that everyone had given up on me, I was still worth the investment and had more to offer education.

Each day was a new day, delivering a new challenge. The students persevered, and so did I. Alberto would be late getting to class, and most days it was obvious he was under the influence. In good conscience, I refused to abstain from commenting; when we met at the door to the rickety portable, I continued to explain that arriving late and being high on marijuana weren't things that were going to assist him in becoming successful. He would give that "aw shucks" grin and proclaim the same thing again and again: "Miss, you know I don't mean it; I won't be tardy tomorrow." Still, he wasn't getting off easy and I insisted that he understand that there were consequences and repercussions for everything; so as punishment and incentive, I would assign him a smaller part in the production and threaten to "fire him" if things got to that. He was still struggling with reading and English as a 17 year old. The Individualized Education Plans and strategies from his Special Education and English for Speakers of Other Languages documents never really met his needs. He avoided learning activities as often as he could to avoid the embarrassment and shame he felt from failure.

Alberto grew that year, and as time passed, he elaborated more and more about his desire to change and to become successful in all areas of his life. He had been in Exceptional Student Education/Special Education for the bulk of his school career, and was still struggling to be fluent in both English and Spanish. We worked hard together to scaffold his learning and support him academically so he could master skills and increase in achievement. His family situation changed often, so as the "man" of the house, he wanted to find a way to protect and preserve whatever sense of normalcy his little brothers and sisters had. Sometimes when the pain was so great, he reached out to find something to numb his feelings. Over time, he reached more and more for marijuana to assist him in managing the raging emotions inside. It worked for a while, but then it turned on him.

Alberto proclaimed that he was embarking on change. He was attending church, and planned to discontinue smoking marijuana; he knew it was detrimental, and he knew it would only lead to further difficulties and chaos. I encouraged and supported him to continue his quest to evolve into all the things he wanted to become.

As the year came to a close, I had struggled tremendously and was still uncertain what direction to take for the next school year. The experiences had been rewarding but exhausting. Was it time to go, or was the next step to come back and do it all over again for a different "Alberto"? The summer would provide some much needed rejuvenation and recovery, and a chance to finally get my own health and life in order. It wasn't long before I got my answer to that question.

As I sat in the physician's office that June for my cancer follow up appointment, I leafed through the newspapers to pass the time; waiting for an hour could seem like forever without something interesting to engage my thoughts. This was a luxury that no teacher could ever afford while working in the classroom.

As I rifled through the local section, a striking headline dumbfounded me: "Dope deal turns deadly—Man shot over $2.00!" *Wow*, I thought, *that is crazy. What is this world coming to?* As I continued reading, I froze and immediately stopped breathing. The report described two boys, ages seventeen and fifteen, who had conducted a drug transaction where the purchaser shorted the dealer $2.00, so the dealer pulled out a gun and shot the victim directly in the face. On the way to the hospital, the victim bled profusely and told the driver to drive as quickly as possible *before it was too late*. Alberto didn't make it.

This was one of the most heartbreaking and gut-wrenching moments in my educational career. It is important for me to tell the story to encourage other like-minded youth workers to trust their gut and intervene as often as possible.

Thank you, Alberto! I am so sad that you lost your life here on earth. A couple of months before this tragedy, I knew that Frank had a gun in the classroom. I tried to tell the administration and security team that we had to get him some help. I even told Frank to get his life together the day that he withdrew from class on his way to rehab. They all continued to tell me that I shouldn't be so dramatic and that I should just mind my own business and stay in my classroom since nobody cares anyway. I have used your story several times to keep it real for students I encounter who argue with me about weed not being potentially problematic, students who tell me they will worry about the future later, and teachers who tell me that you should just look the other way.

Your Mission: Let yourself be right where you are. Most teachers feel such a strong need to "pretend" that they know what they are doing but have gotten very little, if any, training on the nuances, depth, and rigor necessary for student achievement to occur. Give yourself permission to say you don't know, and do research and stay open to learning the art and science of your craft to support your students. Most importantly, start trusting your gut feelings and act on them as often as you can.

Here are the rough draft questions I designed as part of the consulting interview process. They leave a lot to be desired but were a start for me learning to design and develop test type questions for student practice.

Answer the following questions based on the passage "Before It's Too Late."

Standard: R100506: Explain how literary techniques, including foreshadowing and flashback, are used to shape the plot of a literary text.

1. In the third paragraph, the author states that the teacher "reflected back on that story often, and it gave her tremendous comfort in the dark times from which she had recently emerged." How does this example of flashback contribute to the plot of the story?
     A. to demonstrate that Alberto was going through dark times
     *B. to demonstrate that the teacher was also struggling
     C. to demonstrate the hopefulness of the situation
     D. to demonstrate that it might be too late

Standard: R100510: Describe the effect of using sound devices in literary text.

2. "The challenge for his teacher was the same every day: unravel all the discouragement and disillusionment students frequently felt while quickly diagnosing what each would need to be engaged, empowered, and encouraged for that particular day." The author uses the alliteration of *engaged, empowered,* and *encouraged* to influence and appeal to the reader's emotions. Which best describes the mood the author was trying to convey?
     A. The author was attempting to convey hopeless mood.
     B. The author was attempting to convey a rushed mood.
     *C. The author was attempting to convey a hopeful mood.
     D. The author was attempting to convey an angry mood.

45

Standard: R100302: Comprehension strategies: Answer literal, inferential, evaluative, and synthesizing questions to demonstrate comprehension of grade-appropriate print texts and electronic and visual media.

3. Which of the following is the best statement of the plot of this passage?
   A. A student and teacher meet to plan out the year's activities.
   B. A student and teacher meet to develop a plan for instruction to pass an exam.
   C. Alberto develops a plan to change his life and influence those around him.
   *D. The teacher develops a plan to assist and influence the future success of students.

Standard: R100405: Analyze the author's implicit and explicit argument, perspective, or viewpoint in the text.

4. What is a probable reason that the author chose to end the story in the way that she did?
   *A. The author wanted to allow readers the chance to see that not everything has a clear beginning and ending point.
   B. The author wanted the readers to finish the story in their own way.
   C. The author wanted to provide several alternate endings in a series about students.
   D. The author wanted Alberto to still be here to finish the story.

Standard: R100501: Compare and contrast the author's use of direct and indirect characterization, and ways in which characters reveal traits about themselves, including dialect, dramatic monologues, and soliloquies.

5. What conflicts and factors influenced Alberto's untimely death? Use details from the passage to support your answer.

_____

_____

_____

_____

_____

_____

_____

_____

_____

_____

A two-point answer may include the following:

Alberto's untimely death was influenced by a variety of internal and external conflicts and factors. According to the text, Alberto's family situation changed often, and he was expected to be the "man" of the house and protect and provide for his siblings, so the external societal and family pressures influenced his choices at times. In addition, the passage also states that Alberto informed the teacher that he was stopping smoking marijuana because he knew it was detrimental and would lead to chaos. This internal conflict lets the reader know that Alfredo's values and morals conflicted with his behavior.

Additional conflicts include: Alfredo's bilingual struggles— man vs. society: Alberto's Exceptional student education status— man vs. society, man vs. self, etc.

Instructional Implications

1. **What**—*What do I want to do? Which students are fighting the archenemy from this chapter?* Describe your mission around this issue:

    _____

    _____

    _____

2. **How**—*How will I get there and what do I need?* Review the super-HERO solutions/resources provided:
    - "Grade 3 Blended NGSSS and CCSS Question Task Cards"
      http://languageartsreading.dadeschools.net/pdf/ElementaryDocuments/
      Intermediate/NGSSS_CCSS_Blended_TaskCards_G3.pdf
    - Common Core State Standards Initiative
      http://www.corestandards.org/the-standardsCommon Core links
    - National Center for Learning Disabilities
      http://www.ncld.org/types-learning-disabilities/what-is-ld?gclid=
      CIO5   OL7boCFRES7AodEiMA3w

3. **Examine**—*Am I a super-HERO in this situation?* Evaluate your instructional and classroom-management behaviors to determine if they fit in with education super-HERO qualities:
    - **H:** Do my actions/behaviors *help*, not *hinder*?
    - **E:** Do my actions/behaviors *engage*, not *exclude*?
    - **R:** Do my actions/behaviors *resuscitate*, not *ruin*?
    - **O:** Do my actions/behaviors *overjoy*, not *obliterate*?

4. **Conclusion**—*How will I determine the results?* Gather data and anecdotal records to measure possible impact or modifications to make on attendance rates, behavior referrals, academic progress, parent involvement, etc.:

    _____

    _____

    _____

5. **Next Steps**—*What will I do if it didn't work?* List other like-minded individuals to collaborate with who will encourage and support you on your journey:

_____

_____

_____

6. **Celebrate**—*What went right this time?* Jot down your small successes here and document them in your own chapter at the back of the book:

_____

_____

_____

> *No farewell words were spoken, no time to say goodbye.*
> *You were gone before we knew it, and only God knows why.*
> *—Author unknown*

CHAPTER 9

Real eyes. Realize. Real lies.

Jarett, Fighting Contempt

- **The Motto:** Timbuk 3's "The Future's So Bright, I Gotta Wear Shades"—these lyrics describe how the group envisions their future. Our job in working with kids requires that we look beyond the outside of the child to get to the good inside so that students can see their future as bright!
- **The Sidekick:** Jarett
- **The Archenemy:** Contempt
- **The Kryptonite:** Preconceived notions, limited vision, lack of sensitivity and cultural awareness
- **The Super-HERO Lesson:** Never give up on a child!
- **Social Emotional Learning Competency: Self awareness**

"You should start a charter school," several people told me. After I had a good laugh, I told them the truth: at that point in my career, I didn't want anything to do with public education. It had proven to me repeatedly that it was not about the kids and what they needed. My tutoring company had been very successful, but the economic impact of 9/11 left me floundering and in fear of what would happen to me as a single mom the next time something like that happened.

So after a few different people approached me with the charter concept, I considered that it might be a sustainable way to help kids and families in a different way. After I met with a consultant who specialized in writing and putting together charters, I felt more open to the idea and got to work on my part. I would write the curriculum and academic portions as well as the mission and vision. The school would be designed as an at-risk middle school using hands-on learning, positive school climate, and personalized attention. A friend of mine was a professional football player, and I talked with him about how he could play a role in this venture. He could be the "founder" and help with fundraising and notoriety for the school, and I would work on the operations and education and serve as the principal. He liked it and agreed to move forward.

I networked and ran myself ragged trying to keep my tutoring company up and running and to get all the necessary approvals, supplies, staff, and students for a successful opening. The first class of students will always be incredibly special to me as this truly was a labor of love. Many of them had not performed well in traditional schools and needed a place to "start over" and get things right. I just knew that these kids were going to be successful in their work with our school. Each one brought a unique perspective and contributed to our school climate in different ways.

Jarett was one of my founding students, and he hadn't been able to get things right in quite a while. His parents were divorced but were working together to try to get Jarett the help he needed in his 8th grade year before he got into high school. They told me right away that he had been kicked out of his other school—the teachers felt that he had ADD and he didn't work up to his potential—and they were pretty much done with him and the frustration. He knew that every adult he was dealing with had just about given up on him and didn't want to be bothered.

Jarett was a good-looking kid with a mischievous grin. I liked him immediately! His experiences seemed similar to my own growing up, and it seemed he just needed someone to believe in him and *see* him for all the good he had inside. I definitely wanted to help him view his future with bright eyes and optimism.

He started off with my new teachers as the ultimate class clown. He made silly jokes, drew inappropriate pictures of the teachers, fashioned weapons out of paper clips, and all-around just seemed to wreak havoc with his attentional issues and mischief. My poor teachers didn't seem to have the resiliency to deal with Jarett and about eight other boys in the school who had extra needs. They were getting burned out and negative pretty quickly into the year.

So I changed the structure of the school and set up a behavior room with me as the teacher. I was actually very angry inside; I knew it would be so easy to help these boys and get them on track, but the teachers couldn't seem to see the good these young men had to offer our school. We started our class with a behavior incentive program: you earned points to get prizes, eat lunch with the other students, and eventually get out of my behavior program. My driving force in this setting, as in most of all my later classrooms, was to constantly accentuate the positive and keep shaping and molding the students' behaviors and academics so that their self-esteem would get a much-needed boost and their achievement and efficacy would increase.

Jarett was one of my stars almost immediately. He thrived on positive encouragement and loved earning the Frappuccino drinks I had for prizes. We worked together and kept things moving and growing as we went. In the meantime, I was lucky enough to hire some additional help. A former administrator of a juvenile-justice facility came onboard and took some of the inordinate number of tasks I had placed on myself. We were able to work together to infuse the staff with positive support and have all the boys mainstream into the regular classes after a couple of weeks.

The new employee had a restorative justice and therapeutic background, and things really took off in amazing directions as we teamed up as super-HERO twin powers. His male presence, as well as his African-American heritage, was a true godsend for the students. He was an exemplary role model, hilarious, and an intelligent teacher who impacted the whole culture and climate of the school. He taught them ways to start rectifying the wrongs they had done in the past and joined right in with my philosophy of empowering students to engage and enlighten them.

Jarett and some of the other boys held on to their resistance at first. They thought our Titan Town Hall meetings in the morning were for sissies. They couldn't believe we would actually hold them accountable for all things in the school, including giving tours to prospective students, tutoring other kids, running a student-run restaurant, and even monitoring and fixing the bathrooms if there was a clog or some mishap from playing around in the facility. As my partner taught them, "It's *your* school, we just work here." As we infused empowerment and ownership across the entire school day, things continued to get better. Slowly but surely, the students started to see things differently and embrace some of the things that were happening.

Jarett was succeeding and uttered a profound statement that never left me: he wished that Christmas break wasn't so long and asked if we could please have school open up and come there during the break. It felt so good to have someone *see* him for his worth; spending two weeks with his family and their vision of him left him feeling terrible inside. It sure affirmed for me that we were on the right track. As the year progressed, students would struggle and succeed in a variety of ways. There were a series of events that I remember that were profound and important about my learning process and Jarett's development into a young man.

One day, as they were headed out to recess, he and another boy were playing and Jarett pushed the kid into the wall, and it collapsed. These two boys had taken so much ownership in the school that before I even knew about the incident, they came to me and explained that Jarett would bring in the materials and fix it the next day. We discovered he was very talented when working with his hands and mechanics, so he ended up doing a better patching and painting job than a professional might have done.

Later that year, my partner and I had to bring Jarett and his parents into a conference about smoking pot. With his treatment for ADD, it didn't make sense and would be a potentially life-threatening problem if he didn't stop. He really didn't buy it much but had a great deal of respect for us and smiled and listened with half an ear. We treated him with concern, care, and honesty.

At one point in the year he became my security guard so that I could help him understand that his ADD traits were a gift … and all the trouble he had gotten into in the past would now make him an amazing security specialist. No one could lie or trick him. He embraced it the best he could while still maintaining a cool front for his peers.

He even used his elevated status to ask to accompany my partner and I while we presented at a local middle-school conference with our training, "The day the kids took over the school …" When his former teachers saw Jarett up there with us during the presentation, their mouths gaped open and they even stood up and said that they couldn't believe that it was the same student. I secretly winked at Jarett and told him one of my new favorite mantras: "Success is the best revenge." He had intuitively known with his "real eyes" that they believed he would never make it because they thought he was just a "bad kid".

Jarett has stayed in touch over the years and has moved out of Florida to get another fresh start. He is an incredible and amazing young man, and I am so thankful for the opportunity to watch him grow and support him in any way that I am able. Heck, one day I was struggling emotionally and posted on my Facebook that I just want to give up … and the best advice I got back was from Jarett! He said:

> "It goes both ways Lori, and you already know that, you are that
> Mr. Right woman. (lol) You're always right, you thought you were

wrong once … . but you were wrong … =) Of course you should continue to feed people positive feedback and continue to uplift their feelings … but it feels nice to have it returned and maybe that's why you're even posting this about feeling like you want to give up … because maybe no one shows love and appreciation for what you do and or say to them. … So, hey, I say keep killing them with kindness … =) You know I love you and I hope all is well … I'm going to FL Wednesday for Thanksgiving, then coming back to Connecticut … if you're in the area I'd love to catch up."

Thank you, Jarett! You encouraged and inspired me during those difficult days through the initial stages of the charter school and later in my darkness on Facebook. You "buying in" and truly trusting me and my vision kept me going on the days when it seemed like I was spinning my wheels and not helping anyone, anywhere! I am honored to have worked with you in your educational journey.

Your Mission: Find the "negative leader" in your classroom and help him or her embrace his or her inner strengths with courage. The student is basically already in charge of the classroom ambience, so find a positive way to include him or her in the structure and setup of the classroom. It may take time, but when you put the student in a position of responsibility and offer encouragement, you will more than likely find that he or she is truly your best ally and can make profound and important strides with the rest of the students in your class.

Instructional Implications

1. **What**—*What do I want to do? Which students are fighting the archenemy from this chapter?* Describe your mission around this issue:

   _____

   _____

   _____

2. **How**—*How will I get there and what do I need?* Review the super-HERO solutions/resources provided:
   - "Students as Contributors: The Digital Learning Farm" http://novemberlearning.com/educational-resources-for-educators/ teaching-and-learning-articles/students-as-contributors-the-digital-learning-farm/
   - Strategies for Empowering Students http://urbanext.illinois.edu/ce/strat-index.html

3. **Examine**—*Am I a super-HERO in this situation?* Evaluate your instructional and classroom-management behaviors to determine if they fit in with education super-HERO qualities:
   - **H:** Do your actions/behaviors *help*, not *hinder*?
   - **E:** Do your actions/behaviors *engage*, not *exclude*?
   - **R:** Do your actions/behaviors *resuscitate*, not *ruin*?
   - **O:** Do your actions/behaviors *overjoy*, not *obliterate*?

4. **Conclusion**—*How will I determine the results?* Gather data and anecdotal records to measure possible impact or modifications to make on attendance rates, behavior referrals, academic progress, parent involvement, etc.:

   _____

   _____

   _____

5. **Next Steps**—*What will I do if it didn't work?* List other like-minded individuals to collaborate with who will encourage and support you on your journey:

   _____

   _____

   _____

6. **Celebrate**—*What went right this time?* Jot down your small successes here and document them in your own chapter at the back of the book:

_____

_____

_____

> *A teacher affects eternity; he can never tell*
> *where his influence stops.*—*Henry B. Adams*

CHAPTER 10

Born this Way

Jonathan, Fighting for Smart Students

- **The Motto:** The lyrics from Lady Gaga's hit, "Born this Way"--discuss loving who you are no matter what outside circumstances look like at times. Her lyrics touch deeply on LGBTQ issues and racism that often leave kids outcast, bullied, or teased.
- **The Sidekick:** Jonathan
- **The Archenemy:** Differences, Prejudice, Racism
- **The Kryptonite:** Stereotypes, Puberty, "culture shock", legislation
- **Super-HERO Lesson:** Differentiation is for *all* students.
- **Social Emotional Learning Competency: Self-management**

There are many different types of students we encounter as we enter today's twenty-first-century classrooms. The students who are quiet, prepared, and ready to learn can often suffer at the hands of the loud, unruly students who get most of the teacher's attention.

Jonathan and his family had just moved to South Florida from a relatively small town in Pennsylvania. He was a quiet, kind, and intelligent young man who was experiencing a great deal of culture shock in all the ways that South Florida and its perpetual transience can bring. His parents were very involved and also very scared of the "bad" kids Jonathan and his younger sister would encounter in the public school they were zoned to attend.

The transition had been tricky, and the whole family was looking for a place to fit in. They honed in on our ad for a small, supportive environment and inquired almost immediately. They were so sure that they wanted somewhere safe that they managed to overlook our mission statement of supporting struggling learners and for those who weren't successful in other schools—or just interpret it in a way that would include their kids.

I'm not sure how they felt when they were at the initial orientation, but later his mother did whisper quietly to me that, "They're black," referring to the majority of the student population. I tried not to be offended and accepted that it was most certainly a big change for her ... but with my ferocious protective feelings for these kids, I was pretty angry and upset. They instinctively knew that both Jonathan and his sister had many of the characteristics of students who are typically bullied. What none of us realized is that Jonathan was also dealing with questions about his sexual orientation and how come to terms with all that might entail.

As the charter school got up and running, I had such a tremendous amount of pressure and responsibility that I knew deep inside that I couldn't go on working 16 hours a day, 7 days a week and continue to teach full time and run the school full time. I knew that the students needed me, but I also knew that I couldn't continue to do it alone. In the tyranny of the moment, it was so easy to overlook Jonathan with his quiet demeanor. In time, as the stress increased and many of the students were not responding to the many positive behavior interventions and support, I struck upon the one thing I could get up in the morning for: Jonathan. He would always have his homework, would always be prepared, and would always pay attention. So, in the midst of the insanity, I would look Jonathan dead in the eye and tell him that even if no one else listened, I knew he wanted to learn, and I was going to get up every day and come to teach him. Well, of course, this pissed the other students off—and it turned out to be a lucky stroke of genius and behavior intervention on my part.

Later, it was evident that Jonathan and several of the other students needed more advanced and differentiated work, so as I explored options for them. I came up with the idea to partner/contract/provide advanced math courses that would earn them high-school credit through the Florida Virtual School. Who knew that this was actually coming later in the legislation?

Thank you, Jonathan! You kept me going when just about nothing else could. Some days it felt nearly impossible to get up and face all the hurdles of operating, managing, and teaching full-time in a charter school, but knowing you wanted to learn and deserved to have a good teacher was just the right motivation to get me moving. I am honored to have stood in the gap with you as you transitioned to South Florida and then on to what I am sure was an exceptional high school and college career.

I connected with Jonathan recently, and here was his response after reading his chapter:

> Wow, it's interesting how your point of view influenced so much of the student and academic life at Touchdowns4Life. I must say, I was so shy and reserved at that time that I hardly took any notice that I was in any way or form a driving force for you to continue on with the hard days, so I feel very blessed that I was able to do that. So when we first came to the school I actually didn't really notice that most of the kids were black. That wasn't a determining factor in the way that I saw things, but it definitely was for my parents. Different generation, different environment growing up (we came from a small town that was almost entirely white and mountain-esque). What struck me was the lack of respect or lack of interest in school and learning. My mom was always reading books and I completely took that on after her. She was a driving force (as well as my father) in gathering ideas, understanding the world around me, and never judging someone before their actions came.
>
> I was dealing with quite a bit back then. I was realizing that I was not a "heterosexual" or straight, we were moving to a new place that was incredibly different than I grew up in, and I wanted to do the best I could to make up for "faults" I imagined I had. So ... the only way to do that was to throw myself into school work and make the best of what I had. I didn't want anyone to notice me (lest they find out that I was not straight or that I wasn't acting in a stereotypical, masculine middle school way [loud, rambunctious, obnoxious]), I didn't want anyone to pick up on my different skin tone, I didn't want anyone to pick up on my nerdy demeanor or my love of school. This is where I thought ... If I'm having a hard time with my peers, I can only imagine what my teachers felt. And why not make them feel like at least one of us is listening? Because we all were in our own ways ... Some of us just didn't know how to ask for the support and help we needed.
>
> And so we slowly created a small group of us who wanted to learn and be there. We wanted to create an environment where we could all talk and get along, so that's where our little "clique" (I use that word for what the group appeared to be and looked like, but it gives a rather negative connotation ...) formed. And things went from there.
>
> You were probably one of the few influential people in my life, even if I was scared out of my wits to even talk with you back then.

One of those power differentials that existed I guess. You were one of the few people who could completely run that school, and I truly wish you would have stayed because what happened after you left was a monopolization rather than a learning institute. Middle school is a defining period in someone's life and even though I was going through complete shit, you definitely pushed me beyond expectations, and I definitely attribute my placement at the University of Miami, soon to be graduating with honors, to your guidance.

I know you touched on the idea of the virtual school, and although I hated taking it online, I absolutely need to thank you for offering that to us in middle school. That was an amazing help to myself and made me feel much more prepared for 9th grade math. I don't agree with all high school students taking at least one class, and I imagine for some it would be counterproductive, but the fact that you allowed that option was amazing.

I apologize for being so late with this, I'm currently starting up a huge project for graduation from the UM and I've been all over. If you need more details, feel free to ask.

Your Mission: Find out what blended and online learning options are available for your students. The current mandate in Florida dictates that all high-school freshmen for the class of 2015 must take at least one of their courses through the Florida Virtual School.

Instructional Implications

1. **What**—*What do I want to do? Which students are fighting the archenemy from this chapter?* Describe your mission around this issue:

   _____

   _____

   _____

2. **How**—*How will I get there and what do I need?* Review the super-HERO solutions/resources provided:
   - Florida Virtual School
     flvs.net
   - New Classrooms: Blended learning
     www.newclassrooms.org/index.html

3. **Examine**—*Am I a super-HERO in this situation?* Evaluate your instructional and classroom-management behaviors to determine if they fit in with education super-HERO qualities:
   - **H:** Do your actions/behaviors *help*, not *hinder*?
   - **E:** Do your actions/behaviors *engage*, not *exclude*?
   - **R:** Do your actions/behaviors *resuscitate*, not *ruin*?
   - **O:** Do your actions/behaviors *overjoy*, not *obliterate*?

4. **Conclusion**—*How will I determine the results?* Gather data and anecdotal records to measure possible impact or modifications to make on attendance rates, behavior referrals, academic progress, parent involvement, etc.:

   _____

   _____

   _____

5. **Next Steps**—*What will I do if it didn't work?* List other like-minded individuals to collaborate with who will encourage and support you on your journey:

   _____

   _____

   _____

6. **Celebrate**—*What went right this time?* Jot down your small successes here and document them in your own chapter at the back of the book:

_____

_____

_____

> *One who gains strength by overcoming obstacles possesses the only strength which can overcome adversity.—Albert Schweitzer*

CHAPTER 11

This Is the Life for Me..

Teneshia, Fighting Gangs

- **The Motto:** Trick Daddy's "I'm a Thug"—these song lyrics describe not knowing what will happen from one day to the next and finding some stability and security in those folks who are around you and support you: even if they are gangs.
- **The Sidekick:** Teneshia
- **The Archenemy:** Gangs
- **The Kryptonite:** Family rules, poverty
- **The Super-HERO Lesson:** All students need a vision.
- **Social Emotional Learning Competency: Relationship skills**

They came to us from one of the notoriously "bad" schools near our site. They had school record folders that were as thick as a book, with "issues" in behavior, learning, attendance, and suspensions that we never did open. We looked 13 year old Teneshia and her brother Trevor in the eye and said, "Welcome to your new home school."

Both of them were leery, and in the first few days, Teneshia often kept her head down on her desk, sleeping. Trevor shook his dreadlocks loose several times a day and kept a low profile. Our students had already embraced the culture of welcoming new kids and had already given Teneshia and Trevor a tour, sat next to them during our morning announcements, and gave them space to get used to the way they did things at *their school*.

Our charter was written and designed to support struggling students and provide wrap around services in all areas of their lives to help them succeed. We had to develop many protocols and procedures that year. Our uniform policy was an important part of our environment as some of our kids had struggled in the past and had even taken weapons to school. The safety and security feature of the shirt tucked in and belted was a surefire way to agitate the middle-school kids, but it was done with care, dignity, and respect. We allowed families to purchase plain shirts from Walmart that would fit in their budget, rather than demanding they buy a specially designed logo shirt. We also gave great care in avoiding the red and blue colors often associated with gangs. Our Friday shirt was the color of the Miami Dolphins because my football player friend Terry Kirby had played for them and tried to get them to support our non-profit and projects, Touchdowns4Life.

As I was teaching, I always walked around the room, constantly monitoring and giving positive feedback on the students' performance and behaviors. When I would go by Teneshia, I would offer an "olive branch" of sorts and rub her back a little bit and tell her that she needed to wake up and that if she needed to go wash her face to stay awake, she was welcome to go to the bathroom. I guess it took her by surprise that I didn't yell, demean, or threaten her to try to get her to pay attention.

Through the corner of my eye, I could see she was starting to listen during my reading class. Every chance I got, I went by her area and gave as much positive feedback as I could. Over time, she seemed to relax and give herself permission to enjoy the class and the learning centers we were using. Later, she loved for me to read out loud, and she would ask me often if we could all read together and she could read out loud too. It was very touching and I felt pretty proud that she seemed to be excited about learning.

Her brother, Trevor, was quiet but deliberate. As I got more involved with his work and behavior, I could see quickly that he had significant learning gaps that had to be fixed in a myriad of ways. I did several immediate interventions to his curriculum, grouping, and class setting to try to help him find a way to build success on the little reading skills he did have at the time.

Part of the charter that I wrote was the academic part. In doing so, I included learning centers as a legitimate and important way to continue to facilitate student learning even though most schools restrict those activities to elementary-school settings. The Middle Grades Reform Act that passed later actually promoted this idea for best practices. The students had mixed emotions until they began to get the opportunity to extend and enhance their learning in some pretty cool ways. We did soap carvings for our unit on Egypt, had a student-run restaurant for our unit on Italy, and had a great lesson on careers and language arts by making a cereal-box timeline of goals, dreams, and future paths.

The risks that Teneshia and Trevor took while they did that project were astounding; they didn't even realize the importance of what they communicated to my partner and I through their pictures and descriptions. Trevor put as his future a picture of his older brother who was a convicted gang member, and Teneshia put her mother who had ten biological children and struggled repeatedly to not just get caught up, but to stop the monthly backslide into a pit. We were so moved by their projects that we amped up our efforts to push harder and faster to help the kids, (and especially Teneshia and Trevor), understand the impact of their decisions and the incredibly serious consequences of any and all decisions they made. They could get out and we could help them change their trajectory!

It was at about that time that our Titan Town Hall was conceived. One of our students had "stolen" his grandmother's car while she was attending our parent-teacher and board-member meeting. As he was speeding down the nearby street, he rear-ended another car and injured the girl who had gone with him on this little joyride. There were kids outside who saw them leave, and when they got back, all the kids quietly snuck back into the meeting as it was wrapping up. When Roberto's grandmother was leaving, she saw that her car was wrecked, and most of the staff from the school were quick to get involved. As the story unfolded, the police were called, Roberto's probation was revoked, and he left in handcuffs while my partner filmed the whole thing. We planned to show it to the kids the next day, but as I lay awake sick inside that night, a better thought came to mind.

That morning, my partner and I set up our big room with desks put together to resemble a coffin and Roberto's backpack on top of them. We had a makeshift funeral and began an interrogation/trial of the students who had watched Roberto drive off. My partner was as dramatic as I was, and we questioned, probed, pushed, and reiterated the idea that you are guilty when you *don't* tell or intervene in a situation. A couple of the older boys went ahead and took the "stand," and even though they were prodded to take ownership, they came back definitive that they would not be a snitch, no matter what.

As my partner's anger grew, I made the students look and think about the "coffin." My partner yelled out and said, "If it means someone might die, who wants to be a snitch?" No hands raised, and all was quiet for a few minutes. When he asked the question again, Teneshia stood up loud and proud and said, "I do! I am tired of people I love dying, and I want to be a snitch if it means they will live." I thought my partner was going to cry. He recovered quickly and appointed Teneshia our new judge of the Titan Trial. Having a tough young lady like that stand up and embrace a different set of rules was awe-inspiring and pride-producing.

Not only did the school climate shift again for the better, we started the Titan Town Hall meetings from that point on. In a clever play off the ESPN segment, *Jacked up!*, we decided to "call out" students in the morning for the positive and helpful things they had done for each other the day before. The empowerment and enthusiasm that being recognized by their peers gave to the students was exhilarating. As administrators, we quickly jumped in and announced the "starting lineup" of teachers each morning and gave them public recognition as well.

As the days moved on, I got closer to Teneshia and Trevor and learned so much more about their day-to-day life. Their mother was in over her head with ten children and moved often in the middle of the night to avoid the landlord. One early morning, Teneshia called to let me know that she and Trevor weren't going to make it in to school. They had moved in the night to avoid the landlord and they didn't have their uniforms ready. I immediately told her that if she could get to school, I would make sure they had something good to wear, and we would get through whatever we had to in order to make the day great.

As things at home continued to deteriorate for Teneshia and Trevor, my partner and I brainstormed ways to help the family financially and with other services to help get them moving in the right direction. We weren't able to do enough to assist them, and the family ended up moving on and leaving the school when they couldn't find transportation anymore.

I stayed in touch with the kids for a while via phone. Their lives moved back into a path similar to the one they were on when they came to us. They were quickly accused of fighting, crimes, and troublemaking, and the last time I talked to Teneshia, she told me they had both been expelled from school and were trying to find a way to get their GED. It devastated me in so many ways, and I felt so inept at having such a limited window of opportunity to help them change their circumstances.

Thank you Teneshia and Trevor! Your bravery, your honesty, and your willingness to trust me to help you made me strong in ways I didn't know I could be at the time. You both meant a great deal to me and my hope for you is that the time you spent with me comforted you in the middle of your "storm".

Your Mission: Try a new approach with a student who seems to be defiant or disengaged. There are often so many external situations going on in their lives. They may need you to care for them in a different way than they are accustomed to so that they may eventually let their guard down enough to learn and thrive in your classroom.

Instructional Implications

1. **What**—*What do I want to do? Which students are fighting the archenemy from this chapter?* Describe your mission around this issue:

   _____

   _____

   _____

2. **How**—*How will I get there and what do I need?* Review the super-HERO solutions/resources provided:
   - Learning centers in middle school
     http://www.iste.org/docs/excerpts/DIFF68-excerpt.pdf
   - Resiliency in struggling students
     http://www.scholarcentric.com/
   - Classroom meetings
     https://www.responsiveclassroom.org/sites/default/files/
     mm_overview.pdf

3. **Examine**—*Am I a super-HERO in this situation?* Evaluate your instructional and classroom-management behaviors to determine if they fit in with education super-HERO qualities:
   - **H:** Do your actions/behaviors *help*, not *hinder*?
   - **E:** Do your actions/behaviors *engage*, not *exclude*?
   - **R:** Do your actions/behaviors *resuscitate*, not *ruin*?
   - **O:** Do your actions/behaviors *overjoy*, not *obliterate*?

4. **Conclusion**—*How will I determine the results?* Gather data and anecdotal records to measure possible impact or modifications to make on attendance rates, behavior referrals, academic progress, parent involvement, etc.:

   _____

   _____

   _____

5. **Next Steps**—*What will I do if it didn't work?* List other like-minded individuals to collaborate with who will encourage and support you on your journey:

_____

_____

_____

6. **Celebrate**—*What went right this time?* Jot down your small successes here and document them in your own chapter at the back of the book:

_____

_____

_____

Student: Why you always pressin' me man? You are always ridin' me. Why you always doin' that? (Translation: I have too much going on in my world right now and no idea how to handle it.)

Staff: Because we have high expectations here and know you can do better. (Translation: I believe in you and really see what you have to offer. You are capable of so many great things and I won't give up on you no matter how hard you try to push me away.)

—*YouthBuild Troy*

CHAPTER 12

This Is Why I'm Hot!

Dominick, Fighting Disengagement

- **The Motto:** Mims's "This Is Why I'm Hot"—these lyrics point to the values our youth have; hip hop culture, flashy items, and a life of crime. Dominick was privy to the concept and used this song as part of the film he helped edit and make. However, for many urban school teachers some days it feels like a losing battle to try to convince kids that there really is a better way than the media promotes.
- **The Sidekick:** Dominick
- **The Archenemy:** Disengagement
- **The Kryptonite:** Staff, parents, skills
- **The Super-HERO Lesson:** If they give you lemons … make lemonade!
- **Social Emotional Learning Competency: Self-awareness**

Over and over again, I have said what I strongly suspected was true: it was not the kids I had problems with, it was the adults. Working in high-stress environments takes a toll on even the most positive teachers on the planet, but I had to find a way to keep pushing forward no matter what lunacy was handed to me by the administration, district, other teachers, and sometimes even the office staff.

This particular year brought a series of events that made little, if any, sense for student learning and curriculum. In Florida, as in many other high-stakes testing states, there is a mandate for students to score high enough on the state test to earn their diploma. My classes were designed to help those students who could not pass the high-school exam with high-enough scores. The idea, in and of itself, was probably a good one. Unfortunately, there was little, if any, curriculum, measurement, or benchmarks, and a tremendous amount of misunderstanding of what things would work best. I am happy to say that most of these areas have seen some growth to support struggling high-school readers, but failure is still more rampant than anyone should ever accept.

I took this position in mid-January so the students had not had proper teaching or support for the entire first semester at this critical juncture of their lives. As I went to my portable—the last one in the parking lot, furthest away from the school—I entered a run-down, dirty, and chaos-filled room to start my intensive reading classes. I had learned that it was imperative for students to have ownership of their classroom, so I had brought in cleaning supplies, towels, and construction paper to decorate. I grabbed several of the toughest-looking kids and pleaded with them to help me clean, and then I asked for volunteers to help decorate the room. Several of the students bought in, and the rest gave me direct glares of contempt, confusion, and suspicion.

I pushed up my sleeves and started cleaning, and I gave out some paper to invite the noninvolved students to design a graphic of some type that would represent them. (I am pretty sure I included directions to not put profanity or pornography on it, and I asked them to please try to find a way to not include any gang symbols or something along those lines.)

We started making progress, and the room began to feel a little bit brighter. There was no curriculum or books to teach with, so I started by surveying the kids about what topics they would be interested in and began planning thematic units with the Sunshine State Standards infused in the instruction. They came up with music, teen pregnancy, and several other ideas. We started doing some small-group learning centers and research, and we established some routines and procedures for our class.

About the time we got a week or two into the units, the principal and curriculum specialist came in and dropped off last year's history books for us to read and use for our textbooks. The students had already taken the class the year before, and they were outraged to revisit the same material. I convinced them that since we had to do it, we should take a vote on one of the really cool units and do some projects on it that were similar to what we had started with our thematic units.

I slowly but surely won them over, and they decided on a Vietnam history unit. After we got a couple of weeks into the unit, the curriculum specialist showed up again and said that we were now mandated to do novel study and that every reading class was required to read the selected novels: *Killing Mr. Griffin* and *We Beat the Streets.*

My students, although they were not necessarily diligent in their work most days, were furious that we had to abandon yet a second unit. I was shocked and furious that there was such a lack of communication, consistency, or clarity about instruction for kids who needed it most. But it was the other reading teachers who almost started a mutiny this time. Many of them were truly scared of the students and adamantly declared that they *would not* read a book about a group of kids who planned to kill their English teacher. I kind of chuckled to myself and said, "No problem, my students and I will read it first, and we will share our unit plan with you if you guys can do the same for the other book."

As I started to do research on the novel and lay a foundation, I realized that my ninth- and tenth-grade students were functioning at an independent reading and vocabulary level of about grade 6 or 7. The text presented itself with grade-level vocabulary and chapter lengths, so there was not going to be a way for them to read the text independently. I would have to structure and scaffold all the instruction, plot elements, and vocabulary to support the work.

While I delivered my enthusiastic sales pitch about this incredible book we were going to read, the students rolled their eyes, grumbled, and just all-out balked! I designed some note-taking and vocabulary sheets to guide our initial chapters and read the initial pieces of the book orally for support. I stopped often and tried to utilize a strategy called "Visualize and Verbalize" that would help students strengthen the inference, summarizing, and character-analysis skills that they were lacking for the state test.

It was kind of cool to watch them try to get an idea of the characters and the setting and to have them do some quick nonlinguistic sketches of how they imagined the sections unfolded that we were reading. They struggled considerably, and I continued to probe and question to help them dig deeper into the text. Then it hit me: we would summarize the main ideas of the chapters, draw out scenes, analyze characters, and make a movie of this for the end of the school year.

From there, we had to make lists of jobs, think through the logistics, try out for parts, and gather equipment. The students did get more engaged in the learning process, and they did start to be much more invested in reading.

They still loved me to read it to them out loud for support, so most days I would --read the novel orally, discuss, summarize, question, and prompt— three times in a row for 90 minutes each day. I would get tired even though it was so much fun to see the kids actually *ask* me to read and do our work! Wow. That is a teacher of struggling readers' dream come true.

We had directors, assistant directors, scenery, cameramen, props, costume workers, writers, actors, program designers, decorators, and a myriad of other positions filled, and we were on our way. It was definitely a roller-coaster ride. Several students got suspended from school so we had to replace them, several students got into fights during the filming and we weren't able to complete their scenes, the administration and other teachers were baffled that we didn't seem to be reading anything, and the props, scripts, and other written material had a ton of spelling and grammatical errors.

However, I was fortunate to have a few kids who had strong skills in a variety of areas to help push past some of the weaknesses the others had. One student, Dominick, had been a student at my charter school for two years, and I was so happy to have him in class. He was positive, always ready to learn, and willing to help. He was a respectful and solid young man, and the other students weren't quite sure what to make of him and his enthusiasm for learning and growing. Dominick took it in stride and just kept going. He took the "crappy" parts and activities that no one else really wanted to do.

As we were wrapping up the filming, we had solidified plans for a huge VIP premiere: rolling out the red carpet, selected invitees, food, and a full screening of the movie on the classroom wall. We were due to finish filming with the real security guards from the school late that year, however, the school had to go on lockdown because of some vandalism in the portable classrooms. My students were worried we wouldn't finish in time, so Dominick and some of the others begged the security team to go out with them and finish their scene. They were so savvy, they even wrote the helicopters flying around into the script! Absolute genius.

Dominick took the camera home, revamped and edited, added some trendy cool music to the kidnap scene, and burned off copies of the movie for the other students. He truly saved the day and made something that was good *great*.

The screening day arrived. The kids were excited and anxious to make sure that the one person they got to invite would be allowed to attend. They cleaned, decorated, organized, and walked up the red carpet that led to the portable with pride. Several of the students who had gotten suspended were able to come back and have the "list" at the door, and to serve as security for the event.

The only staff to attend were the two security guards who were in the movie, the reading coach, and one other teacher. The administration, guidance department, and the other eighty-one staff members didn't make it. The rest of the room was full of students, pizza, friends, and camaraderie. I cried, of course, and I couldn't have been prouder of my students. They left that day after they cleaned everything up I heard Chris, one of the directors, tell another student, "You know, that was the only reason I even *came* to school this last month."

That one statement made it all worth it.

Thank you Dominick! Your support and enthusiasm made me laugh, smile, and feel like I was making a difference. It was my favorite part of the day when you came to class and wanted to learn and laugh with me.

I have stayed in touch with Dominick over the years, and when I asked him to tell me what things I should tell other teachers to do in a book, here is what he said:

> Hello Ms. Lori,
>
> I first want to start off by apologizing for my late reply. I have not checked my Facebook inbox in a while. Work has me so tied up you would not believe. I truly hope that I could still be of some assistance to my chapter in your book.
>
> For the few years I have known you, you have impacted my life tremendously. Around the age of 15-16 it was an honor to have you as my principal, mentor, and ninth grade teacher. You have taught me to be an aspiring individual: one who does not give up or throw in the towel on chasing my dreams and goals no matter what obstacles may get in my way. To be an individual that does not care what people think about me or about how cool I look participating and being the smartest student in class. You have showed me just what it takes and to continue to strive for success both in and outside of the classroom. You always separated me from the students that went to school just because they were forced to go there by their parents, and paired me up with other students that pushed themselves to the limit to achieve the best results. You looked out for my best interest in the classroom and out. Thank you keep in touch.

Your Mission: Follow Dominick's advice: Look out for your students' best interests ... in the classroom and out.

Update: I recently was invited to Dominick's wedding and was honored to be asked to give the first toast of the bride and groom. I summarized what I already knew, he and his wife will continue to be super-HERO symbols to many, and it was so refreshing to see the "good guy" win for a change.

Instructional Implications

1. **What**—*What do I want to do? Which students are fighting the archenemy from this chapter?* Describe your mission around this issue:

   _____

   _____

   _____

2. **How**—*How will I get there and what do I need?* Review the super-HERO solutions/resources provided:
   - "Movie-Making in the Classroom"
     http://www.scholastic.com/teachers/top-teaching/2013/03/movie-making-classroom-overview

- "High Schools That Work" and "Making Middle Grades Work"
  http://www.sreb.org/page/1078/high_schools_that_work.html
  http://www.sreb.org/page/1080/making_middle_grades_work.html

3. **Examine**—*Am I a super-HERO in this situation?* Evaluate your instructional and classroom-management behaviors to determine if they fit in with education super-HERO qualities:
   - **H:** Do your actions/behaviors *help*, not *hinder*?
   - **E:** Do your actions/behaviors *engage*, not *exclude*?
   - **R:** Do your actions/behaviors *resuscitate*, not *ruin*?
   - **O:** Do your actions/behaviors *overjoy*, not *obliterate*?

4. **Conclusion**—*How will I determine the results?* Gather data and anecdotal records to measure possible impact or modifications to make on attendance rates, behavior referrals, academic progress, parent involvement, etc.:

   _____

   _____

   _____

5. **Next Steps**—*What will I do if it didn't work?* List other like-minded individuals to collaborate with who will encourage and support you on your journey:

   _____

   _____

   _____

6. **Celebrate**—*What went right this time?* Jot down your small successes here and document them in your own chapter at the back of the book:

   _____

   _____

   _____

I think there are definitely two types of students: the academic kids and the 50 percent who fail. It's very clear to see—it's fact. We're not doing enough for those who fail; they need a more physical, tactile approach, involving people skills, team-building, problem-solving, building things.—Jamie Oliver

CHAPTER 13

I'm Not Afraid

You, Fighting for Students

- **The Motto:** Eminem's "Not Afraid"—these lyrics: I'm not afraid-- to take a stand echo my sentiments in this work. The rapper goes on to say to take my hand and we will walk together through these storms. I hope that these stories have let you know that you are not alone and that you DO make a difference when you put your mind and heart to it.
- **The Sidekick:** You!
- **The Archenemy:** The haters and naysayers
- **The Kryptonite:** Hurt, disillusionment, disbelief, lack of hope
- **The Super-HERO LESSON:** Why not me? Why not you?
- **Social Emotional Learning Competency: All of them: Self-awareness, Self-management, Social Awareness, Relationship skills, and Responsible decision making**

The Story of the Starfish

A young teacher was walking along the ocean and saw a beach on which thousands and thousands of starfish had washed ashore. Further along he sees an old man, walking slowly and stooping often, picking up one starfish after another and tossing each one gently into the ocean.

"Why are you throwing starfish into the ocean?," he asks. "Because the sun is up and the tide is going out and if I don't throw them further in they will die." "But, old man, don't you realize there are miles of beach and starfish all along it! You can't possibly save them all, you can't even save one-tenth of them. In fact, even if you work all day, your efforts won't make any difference at all."

The old man listened calmly and then bent down to pick up another starfish and threw it into the sea. "It made a difference to that one."

Your Mission: It is a classic story about the power of each of us to make a difference in the lives of others. We are here for each other and should seek to help, even in small ways, whenever we can. Throw one starfish back today—even if *you* are the starfish!

Instructional Implications

Document all of your celebrations and notes in your own chapter that follows.

Never doubt the power of a small group of dedicated citizens to change the world. Indeed, it is the only thing that ever has.—Margaret Mead

CHAPTER 14

Your Chapter

- **The Theme Song:**
- **The Sidekick:**
- **The Archenemy:**
- **The Kryptonite:**
- **The Super-HERO Lesson:**
- **Social-Emotional Learning Competency:**

Be on the lookout for:

SOS! Save Our Students-More Solutions
Teachers and Youth workers: You and your student sidekick could be included in our next book! Submit Your Chapter and be considered for our next edition and a $100.00 gift card! Email:saveourstudentsnow@gmail.com

SOS! Saving Our Selves-Student stories
Middle School and High School teachers and students: Every student can gain from reading this book with you in class. To maximize the impact, have your students write and submit their OWN chapter for our series: SOS! Saving Our Selves.

SOS! Save Our Staff-Instructional Coaching and teacher tales
Daily warm-up lessons, classroom kits, social emotional learning products, and other SuperHERO resources!

Join the growing SuperHERO team: We offer training, books, products, and support for schools, non-profits, students, and stakeholders who are fighting the arch-enemies of education.

Website: www.trainourteachers.com
FACEBOOK: S.O.S. Save Our Students
LINKEDIN: Lori Bitar
Twitter:@LoriBitar

I can't wait to hear from you!

PLC/BOOK CLUB DISCUSSION QUESTIONS

INTRODUCTION-My chapter
- What feelings were triggered in you by my honest sharing of my childhood?
- How did your childhood and teen years shape you?
- What is one thing you would be willing to work on from this chapter?

CHAPTER 1-Jermaine
- How do you feel about 'the class clown"?
- What are some effective ways to redirect their behavior to decrease their time off task?
- What is one thing you would be willing to work on from this chapter?

CHAPTER 2-Terry
- What do you know about teaching reading and infusing literacy in your content area?
- How does your current infusion of technology support and interfere with student literacy?
- What is one thing you would be willing to work on from this chapter?

CHAPTER 3-Laura
- What community partners do you already know to connect with for support?
- What teaching challenge did you have that ended up making you a better teacher?
- What is one thing you would be willing to work on from this chapter?

CHAPTER 4-Matt
- What biases do you think prohibit students with ADD from getting the help they need?
- What effective solutions have you used to supplement the whole child approach of diet, exercise, therapy, and medication?
- What is one thing you would be willing to work on from this chapter?

CHAPTER 5-Christian
- What can you say to a colleague who labels a student "bad"?
- What types of motivation and encouragement activities have you used in the mornings to start the day off right?
- What is one thing you would be willing to work on from this chapter?

CHAPTER 6-Danny
- In what ways can you challenge the adults who tell you to look the other way?
- What behavior management techniques have worked well for you?
- What is one thing you would be willing to work on from this chapter?

CHAPTER 7-Michael
- Who can you trust to make sure that your students get the help they need?
- What types of parent support and engagement techniques have you had success with?
- What is one thing you would be willing to work on from this chapter?

CHAPTER 8-Alberto
- What success tips do you have for managing students with an IEP?
- Which best practices are used for test-taking strategies?
- What is one thing you would be willing to work on from this chapter?

CHAPTER 9-Jarett
- What empowering positions do you give your students?
- How can you infuse social emotional learning skills into your day?
- What is one thing you would be willing to work on from this chapter?

CHAPTER 10-Jonathan
- What activities do you use to support your gifted students?

- Can we engage LGBTQ students better in the classroom?
- What is one thing you would be willing to work on from this chapter?

CHAPTER 11-Teneshia

- How have you provided stability for your students who are struggling with poverty?
- What college and career conversations and resources can you use to help students develop a vision?
- What is one thing you would be willing to work on from this chapter?

CHAPTER 12-Dominick

- What project based learning activities can you do to engage students?
- Which school support staff would like to help your students-office, custodial, security?
- What is one thing you would be willing to work on from this chapte